Reclaiming Your Testimony

Reclaiming
Your
Testimony
Your Story and
the Christian Story

R. Lamar Vest
& Steven J. Land

Library of Congress Catalog Card Number: 2001097313
ISBN: 0-87148-547-8
Copyright ©2002 by Pathway Press
Cleveland, Tennessee 37311
All Rights Reserved
Printed in the United States of America

DEDICATION

Affectionately dedicated to our fathers,

B. B. VEST

and

JACK LAND

men whose lives were dynamic visuals of what it means for God's story to truly be the individual's story.

R. Lamar Vest, General Overseer
Church of God

Steven J. Land, Dean of Academics
Church of God Theological Seminary

CONTENTS

PROLOGUE

Reframe your life in such a manner that when you share your testimony, you are, in fact, telling the Christian story or God's story.

A rather odd thing happened when the two of us decided recently to make separate journeys back to our respective hometowns (Steve to Jasper, Alabama, and Lamar to Laurens, South Carolina). We both had big memories of small towns.

Interestingly, houses that loomed large in our memories turned out to be much smaller. Distances were shorter than we remembered. The mental images and significance of these memories were much larger than the actual events or places.

The trips reminded us that the smallest events in our lives can sometimes have the greatest significance. We understood that if either of us could have spoken personally with persons who were contemporary with the unfolding of some of the greatest events in history, chances are we would not have heard them express whether they were for or against the events. They would have been more likely to say, "I really didn't know it was that significant."

Most people who were contemporaries of Jesus went right on working in the fields, tending their flocks and fulfilling their daily routines without ever knowing the significance of His presence among them. Anne Sullivan, the teacher, never really knew that the innumerable hours she spent teaching a deaf, mute and blind Helen Keller would give such hope and inspiration to millions who would later hear the story.

On the negative side, the church deacon in South

Africa who turned Gandhi away from the front door of his church surely did not know his act would have such great significance. How different might the history of India be today if Gandhi had been welcomed into Christian faith and fellowship!

Few who were most socially prominent or publicly visible when we were growing up appeared on our list of most influential persons. Instead, we recalled the real personalities—family, friends, saints of God— those who specifically embodied what it meant to be Christian when we were children. Steve reminisced:

> I remember Marie Jackson, an elderly, mentally handicapped woman living in a low-income housing project. I can still hear her loud praises, reminding me of the public warning siren on top of the Jasper courthouse. I always wondered what this poor, rather unattractive woman had to be so happy about. Frequently, she would use a part of her government check to feed neglected children in the housing projects, or she would invite people such as my family to Sunday lunch.

> When I view life through her eyes, themes that the world considered so important—beauty, wealth, popularity, intelligence—turn out to have much less significance. Today, I can rejoice with her, and all those like her, because God is truly no respecter of persons.

After a pilgrimage to his old home, Lamar said:

> My hometown of Laurens had Jason Compton. Jason drove the milk truck. He was one of the first people who confirmed God's call on my life. Jason wasn't a great teacher, a political figure

or a distinguished writer. So far as I ever knew, he didn't have an educational degree to hang on the wall. But he walked in the light God gave him and he reflected some of that light my way. Jason took me fishing nearly every week when I was a teenager, and he used those occasions to tell me what God put into his heart concerning my life.

When I first started preaching, it was Jason Compton who took me aside after Sunday night service and told me Price's Department Store had a sale on suits. He insisted I needed to go down and talk with the sales clerk. When I went to the store, I found out that Jason had already been there. He had paid for my suit, along with a shirt and matching tie. Jason did that more than once. You think I've forgotten?

Reminiscing on those trips reminded us both that we hadn't always known at the time just which life moment would end up being truly significant. "Judge nothing before the time," Paul tells us in 1 Corinthians 4:5.

He also reminds us: "We know that all things work together for good to those who love God, to those who are the called according to His purpose" (Romans 8:28).

What we knew was that God was at the center of our lives. Looking back, we could see how much His hand was at work . . . in so many ways . . . in so many lives . . . through so many situations. As we talked and shared these stories with one another, more than once we found ourselves with tears in our eyes.

These stories were hallowed stories, springing up out of deep wells of blessings from which we had been drinking for many years. We realized that sometimes we drank unknowingly.

It became obvious that at each of several critical crossroads, we could have gone down another path. There was little doubt in our minds that the wrong choice could have meant death or spiritual ruin just as had happened for a number of our teenage friends.

Our remembering and sharing pointed out graphically for us just how fragile life can be. Yet, through it all, there has always been the gentle, invisible hand of God's divine providence. In prayer, we confessed together the grace of God, and gave worshipful thanks for His mercy and provision.

In addition to the usual childhood and adolescent stories—stories the two of us have in common with millions of others—we also recalled miracles and everyday blessings which shaped our lives. Steve said:

> I was only 5 years old when Dad suffered a near fatal ulcerated hemorrhage in his stomach. I awoke to find blood on the other side of my bed where Dad had been sleeping. There was blood on the bedroom floor. When I found Dad semiconscious in the bathroom, there was blood all over him too.
>
> Thinking back on it I should have been scared, but I wasn't. I remember a sense of peace and a wonderful assurance as I went up to Dad and did what the men always did down at the Jasper Church of God. I put out my hand, touched Dad on the head, and said, "O God, heal my dad in Jesus' name."

And God did just that. Not only was my dad healed, but I came to realize later how the occasion bonded me with Dad in a deep and meaningful way. Neither Dad nor I knew it at the time, but God knew that the two of us would need that bond years later when He called us to an inner-city ministry in the city of Atlanta.

Lamar remembered some of the miracles that helped shape his life:

The church was full and there were no seats for the children. I was sitting on the altar. I watched with eyes wide open as God gloriously healed two men in a single night. One of the men was blind from birth, the other was deaf from birth. What I saw forever shaped my view of the world and what I knew was possible through faith in God. I have never questioned whether the gifts of the Spirit are real because I saw them operate with my own eyes and heard with my own ears. I knew and still know that God performs miracles.

As we talked further, another truth came to light. Equally important for both of us were those occasions when good people suffered and were not healed. They, too, were people of faith. For some reason they were not healed, but they endured and pressed on with gracious trust and quiet dignity. Lamar recalls:

One man I remember well was Brother Demary. He lost his job and was forced to move into an abandoned tenant house. His wife was terminally ill and in the hospital. Brother Demary was plowing one day, trying to prepare a garden for food, when his daughter came running to him in the field. She was yelling that the house was on fire. Breathlessly, she said, "Daddy, it's all burning. We've lost everything." Brother Demary told her and others later, "No, we haven't lost everything. We still have God, and He's more important than things that burn."

All of us have gone through similar stages of human development and spiritual struggles as we grew up. Some have had more hardships than others. Some have had more privileges and blessings than others. We have all lived in different places, during different periods of history, and we have related to many different types of people. The intriguing plots of our lives have a peculiar mix of *time* and *place, persons* and *situations,* all of which give each of us a personally unique sense of identity.

So each of us has a story to tell. Our fingerprints and faces may be different, but we share a common humanity, with common hopes and fears. For Steve and me, flowing through the soil of this rich heritage is the truth of Christian faith in a Pentecostal context. We were both sort of the odd ones in school, since there were not many Pentecostals when we were young.

Growing up Pentecostal meant that, although we were persons like everyone else, we were still somehow different. We were set apart because of those awesome encounters with God and the peculiar commitments, relationships and practices which characterized what it meant to be Pentecostal—laughing, shouting, dancing, weeping, speaking in tongues.

We were also those boys who went to a church where there was no smoking, no drinking of alcohol of any kind, and no going to movies.

We recall early preachers with their teaching charts stretched across the front of the church. We didn't always know what those strange creatures represented, but we knew the end was coming and there were strange "creatures" out there in the spirit world. The message was straightforward and plain: sin was sin; God was God; and judgment was sure and certain.

Much has changed today. Horrible things are still happening in the world—like the slaughter of thousands in the Sudan, the hunger of multitudes in urban ghettos, the widespread abuse of children, the scourge of AIDS, a terrorist attack on big-city skyscrapers. A sophisticated society— and all too often the church—speaks of these things as *unfortunate events* and moves on with a flip of the TV channel. For the most part the church no longer uses those powerful Biblical symbols of the world, the flesh, the devil and the sure judgment of God.

Through the sharing of stories, Steve and I came to understand again that religion was not just a part of our lives: *it was the center of our lives.* We realized how so many of the best of our stories were inextricably bound up in the Church of God story. Each of the wonderful people we remembered had his or her individual story, some tragic and some triumphant, but all together they reflected the church's story.

We shared something in common with Christians everywhere; but, with us, it was more than a string of facts linked to faces and dates. It was truth, eternal truth, *made to burn* with the fire and presence of God.

The purpose of this book is to underscore the importance of personal testimony. We are not referring to the "testimony services" we used to have in church on Wednesday nights, but to the central core of faith that gives every believer identity and furnishes the fuel for witnessing to every individual we meet. This is the essence of relationship with Christ.

There are many stories by which people identify themselves. The normal story we each have about the meaning of life is crucial. If that story for us is the Christian story, then the question becomes, "Do we truly live our lives according to the story? Do other stories compete with the Christian story?"

Out of the story of our lives, the basically understood meaning of our lives, we each construct a worldview. It tells us who we are, to whom we belong, where we are going, and how we are going to get there. The problem most of us have revolves around what we make the center, the core, of all choices and decisions.

Many stories claim to be Christian but prove to be false or contradictory. In today's world it is still possible for someone to say, "My name is Legion," because they live out of so many stories and are driven by so many forces.

The only true answer to this fragmentation of the heart comes through the Cross and one's personal relationship with the Lord of glory. With Him at the center, things fall into place.

When we cease living out the Christian story, we end up being controlled by dry abstractions and man-made rules. These profane, momentary experiences have some semblance of the sacred but are basically mere episodes soon to be forgotten. We end up being one type person at church and then another at home or on the job.

Most people do not come into the Christian life on their own initiative. They come to a new belief through exposure to the testimony of others. Testimony is the essential element of influence. People walk with reference to and live in the presence of the tested and proven things of another soul.

Our testimonies, thus, become a standard by which the needs, feelings, experiences and faith of others are tested. Each rising generation comes with its own set of attributes, some good and some bad. The characteristics of the contemporary generation are both frightening and encouraging. According to research:

- They have all but given up on the American dream, and yet they have a greater global awareness than any generation before them.

- They have massive hidden pain, nearly 50 percent come from divided families, yet they openly search for intimacy.

- They possess a graphic aversion to institutions, and yet they have formed their own establishments of friends or gangs, or of anyone else who will spend time with them.

- They are suspicious of religious extremists, and yet they are searching for transcendent meaning.

- They are skeptical about absolute truth, and yet they are open to the stories of others, hardly ever arguing with their authority.

There has never been a generation more open to the sincere witness of others than this one. People may not be so quick to accept religion and dogma from the professional religionists, but they rarely lift an argument against one's personal testimony. This can be a blessing or a curse, depending on who is witnessing to them.

Unfortunately, many Christians seem to have adopted a pledge of silence as it relates to testimony. This is certainly not the day for Christians to be silent. If this generation is to be won to Jesus, narrative must be recovered. We must be able to repeat in our own terms what we have experienced. We all have our stories and they must be told.

In telling our stories, we interpret ourselves and our experiences while reaffirming that God is available to do the same for others. Unlike other stories, the Christian story is paramount. By its very nature it is designed to be shared with everyone because it is about the God of everyone.

If we fail to give our testimonies, then we don't understand the story sufficiently or we don't really believe it. The explosive power of witnessing through the Holy Spirit cannot long remain in our lives if we fail to publicly share what He has called us to be.

For the Pentecostal, living the Christian life without detection is like trying to explode a bomb in the middle of town without anyone noticing. Those who are filled with the Spirit cannot help but speak those things both seen and heard (see Acts 4:20).

The love of God is the "divine drive" that motivates us to share with others. We don't really have a choice. The issue is absolutely vital. We are God's representatives. To *experience* and *report* is the most fundamental thing a Christian can do. All God asks is that we report, in our own terms, what He has done for us. We are not all evangelists, but we are all witnesses.

Others have stories to tell, of course, but we have the tremendous advantage of knowing the Holy Spirit is present to show the truth of Christ Jesus. As Paul reminded us, the gospel is the power of God unto salvation (Romans 1:16). Thus, we must get the story straight, we must tell it well and often, and we must faithfully persevere in the name of risen Christ, until   all have heard and come to know Him as Lord.

Christian people without a testimony—a story to tell—are a people without a future.

CHAPTER 1

PARADE
OR
PILGRIMAGE?

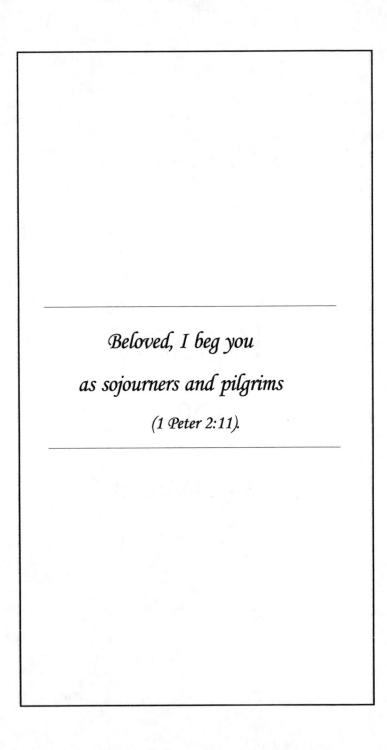

Beloved, I beg you

as sojourners and pilgrims

(1 Peter 2:11).

*I*f we as a church are to recover and maintain a powerful, truthful witness in today's culture, we must decide whether we are *in a parade* or *on a pilgrimage* with God. The two are completely different.

The parade turns us all into competitors and rivals; the pilgrimage transforms us into companions in the journey of life. People in a parade bear witness of their own accomplishments. They have something they want to display. They want to show off their possessions and skills and gaudy floats.

People on pilgrimage bear witness to the mighty acts of God. In a parade, people proclaim how great they are. On a pilgrimage, the saints sing to God "How Great Thou Art."

A parade has no future. Paraders circle a few blocks, do a lot of yelling and cheering, may even receive some token prizes, but they always end up where they started. The crowd disperses. The excitement is over; everyone goes home. There is such meaninglessness, such inherent despair in all this.

THE CHRISTIAN PILGRIMAGE

Why then, one wonders, do we keep inviting our young people to join a parade? Do we not know that sooner or later they will wise up to the fact that we are going to leave them stranded on the curb as life passes them by? If we will listen, this analogy between *parade* and *pilgrimage* has even more to tell us.

A parade requires only *spectators*, but a pilgrimage

requires *participants.* In a pilgrimage, you take everybody with you. If they are too weak to walk, carry them. If they fall, pick them up. If they stray from the path, bring them back. Pilgrims always keep moving because they have a mission and a destination. A parade is a visual, brief and momentary experience. The Christian pilgrimage is a life's journey.

The essential mission of God's people on earth—the church—is to become a servant people who live in covenant relationship with God. Their purpose is not to impress the world with a parade of favorites. All of us are on pilgrimage together.

We are to form relationships so that we can love people as God loves them. We are not called to impart abstract principles for success or effectiveness. Instead, we are to give a witness that invites people into new life.

Being successful doesn't make one a Christian. There are plenty of people who set goals and reach them. But merely being successful or effective is nowhere near the same thing as being Christian. Faithfulness in this task requires far more than selfish achievement.

In their informative book, *Selling Out the Church: The Dangers of Church Marketing,* Philip D. Kenneson and James L. Street share words that should make us think when we are portraying the church of Jesus Christ on earth today. They write:

> Effectiveness is always discerned with respect
> to some agreed-upon goal or purpose. Yet

marketers rarely ever tell us what that goal or purpose is; indeed, they often make it sound as if greater effectiveness is itself the goal . . . in other words, to be an effective market-driven church is nothing other than to keep your consumers happy (and, therefore, present).[1]

We are never going to successfully market the church as a convenient product. There is no way we can fulfill what God has called us to do by hawking our wares like a television infomercial.

Look again at the parade analogy. The parade traditionally displays all kinds of idolatry. Its emphasis seems always to be on brains, brawn, beauty and bucks. A successful parade depends on the same old celebrities—beauty queens, sports stars, movie-sex symbols, the intellectually elite, the wealthy.

Competition is the name of the game being played in "parade" churches. In this competitive atmosphere, everyone is striving to be better than those who preceded them. Individuals ultimately become identified as winners or almost-winners, not as faithful or unfaithful or even as good or bad.

THE MISUNDERSTOOD MESSAGE

Contemporary men and women are adrift in a sea of faces, gathering in the public square, going nowhere. Occasionally they will enter the competition, but more often they merely watch. They have no personal story to tell and thus life has no meaning for them. They have no perceived ultimate destination. Stories may be written about them, but they themselves have no story to tell.

A culture which craves recipes, programs and competition easily embraces human/secular pragmatism. Religion and pragmatism are no strangers. They have paraded together under all sorts of banners, asking such questions as *How does it work? How much does it cost? What's in it for me? Is it really worth the effort?*

The Cult of Pragmatism

Unfortunately, pragmatism has become the key word for many Christians today. As a symbol it is a great time-saver. Pragmatic religion advocates a mentality that permits people to avoid the sacrificial aspects of the gospel and go straight to the asset column.

Pragmatism allows us to play God because we set the rules, establish the objectives and determine the outcome. The pragmatist calls it truth if it works. Because a belief is useful, however, does not necessarily make it true.

The plague of human/secular pragmatism ties religion to a system of consumerism that advertises three hedonistic slogans: *get it, use it* and *enjoy it.* It tells you to find that church where your children will mix and mingle with others from affluent neighborhoods.

Use church contacts to find prospects for your growing business. Enjoy the choirs and the special entertainment features. After all, some of the celebrities are really good and church is far less expensive than the theater. These people represent the pragmatic appeal.

While pragmatism and religion may go hand in hand, pragmatism and true Christianity do not mix easily. Here are some reasons:

- Christianity is a covenant community, not a consumer religion.
- Christianity _has_ a creed, but it _is not_ a creed.
- Christianity follows a set of beliefs, but it is more than a religion.
- Christianity finds its greatest fulfillment in worshiping its God, not in personal gratification.
- Christianity finds its absolutes in the promises of God, not in appealing circumstances.
- Christianity realizes wholeness through relationships, not through successes and possessions.
- Christianity is not meant to be a part of life or apart from life—it is life!

Amazingly, some use their faith to authenticate almost every occurrence in life. One lady said she knew it was God's will for her to purchase a dozen doughnuts, although she was on a strict diet. Her reasoning: "Why else would God allow a parking space to open up in front of the bakery at the exact time the red neon 'Hot Donuts Available' sign came on in the window?"

She conveniently forgot to mention that she circled the block six times before the space became available.

Such petty behavior bears little resemblance to the serious-minded pilgrims who launched Christianity in the first century. Or to the Christians around the world who regularly put their lives on the line for the sake of Christ.

Pragmatism focuses on beliefs that attempt to justify or explain circumstances and give a formula by which benefits can be obtained. It reduces faith to bumper sticker slogans. It speaks disparagingly of doctrines which deal with profound truths—truths hard-won through years of diligent searching and deliberation.

Many seek this utilitarian aspect of religion today. Pragmatism is sometimes welcomed as a colleague of religion because:

- *Function* is deemed much more important than *belief.*
- *Practicality* is considered more essential than *truth.*
- *Validation* is seen as more legitimate than *hope.*
- *Efficiency* is treated as more fundamental than *principle.*

How well it works seems to be what gives the most convincing evidence to the value of religion today. Such religion fits well into the modern concept of consumerism.

The Paralysis of Ambivalence

Consumerism leaves room for buyers' remorse and sometimes encourages it. What happens when you get the product and it doesn't live up to its publicity? What happens when you try to use it and it doesn't work as advertised?

How do you handle it when hurtful circumstances drain away the joy? How do you deal with conflicting emotions? Like all cults, pragmatism never lives up to its promises.

We all know individuals who have been disillusioned by some aspect of their Christian experience. They know what they have heard, but too often what they have been told and what they have experienced are different things.

Legions still fight personal battles with the inner arbiter called *uncertainty*. Most of the time these battles are fought alone, unnoticed, perhaps with a feeling that no one else has ever faced such uncertainties.

Someone who was recently encouraged to attend the "exciting, joyful worship services" at a particular church remarked, "It's difficult to rejoice with others when I've spent so much time crying alone."

Far too many cry alone, struggling to overcome fears and doubts, trying to find that level of confident living which sustains their faith—even when circumstances indicate something has gone wrong.

So many find no sympathetic understanding when they go to church. What they hear on Sunday doesn't seem to relate to what they are experiencing the rest of the week. Grief, tears, suffering and lament are all forced underground.

A humanly pragmatic church has no consolation for, or patience with, such pessimistic things because those things are seen as simply not good for public relations.

The Curse of Carnality

Come to think of it, the Cross may not be good public relations either; but it is essential for salvation. We remain caught up and forced to live in what Stephen L. Carter called "a *secular* culture, devoted to sweet reason."[2] Christianity is more than something to be merely enjoyed. A right relationship with God brings a good feeling, but good feelings are not all there is to being a Christian.

Jesus elevated religion from the realm of good feeling to that of conviction and responsibility. Edith Schaeffer posed some poignant questions on this thought in her book *Affliction* by asking:

> Are Christians meant to be happy all the time?
> Are we meant to be feeling fulfilled all the time?
> Are we looking inward and examining ourselves
> to see whether we know who we are? Is life to
> be a self-centered journey? The ideas that turn
> us in these directions are like false shortcuts
> which lead nowhere but into a blind alley.[3]

Much of what we hear about God today is little more than man's attempt to satisfy religious curiosity. Despite human versions to the contrary, God is not a mainframe computer with all the information and answers stored away, just waiting for humans to tap in and retrieve them.

He is more than the "great Mind of the universe" who designed and created everything, and then just disappeared. God is personal, and He must be approached on that basis.

The gospel of the quick fix is the cry of today. Some turn to Christianity, it seems, in order to get *high* on Jesus. Others have a service station attitude toward religion and church: it is the necessary stopover when their spirits are low and they need a fill-up, or when they are sluggish and need to flush out the rust and the dregs of guilt.

This kind of gospel plays especially well to a "McChurch" culture, something that can provide a quick, drive-through service and immediate miracles.

THE FOLLY OF FOLK RELIGION

There is a great gulf between the God of Biblical faith and the god of modern folk religion.

- The god of folk religion is a God of sentimental love, not holy love. The god of folk religion is treated as "the man upstairs," not as the sovereign God of the universe.

- The god of folk religion is esteemed as an indulgent father who looks the other way when his children sin, not as the eternal, righteous Judge.

- The god of folk religion is the middleman between people and their desire.

- The god of folk religion has molded and crafted a new Jesus with another gospel.

In *Wise Blood,* Flannery O'Connor writes of Hazel Motes, a self-made evangelist who sets out to found his own religion. He calls it "The Church Without Christ," and attempts to portray a new Jesus who would support this religion.

O'Connor seems to have written prophetically of this day when many are promoting a new, human Jesus of culture rather than the divine Jesus of Scripture.[4]

The Crunch of Commercial Christianity

With a note of sadness, John the Beloved wrote, "He came to His own, and His own did not receive Him" (John 1:11). John's words were never more relevant than they are today. No age has been more cut off from the historical Christ, the Messiah, the Christ of Scripture, than ours. There has never been a generation that needed Him more.

One of the infamous creations of our market-driven society is the infomercial. This marketing tool, ostensibly a combination of information and a commercial, is designed to sell a product and to build a clientele.

People are paid to give testimonials to a product, telling, quite naturally, only the good points of the product in order to increase the sales. Individuals in the infomercial are paraded before us with smiling faces and glowing reports. All possible negatives of the product being hawked are hidden in the descriptive small print and the fast sales talk that comes at the end of the program.

The church is not commanded to sell a product or build a clientele. It is not to cover up the demands of true discipleship. The church has a divine mandate. It is on pilgrimage with a message. The church is challenged with the responsibility of building a community of truthful witnesses. Unfortunately, we are too prone to forget. As Kenneson and Street write:

> The church has to be continually reminded that it is not called to feed the hungry, clothe the naked, or visit the imprisoned because it is seeking personal or customer satisfaction, but because the people of God have been called to bear embodied witness to God's "upside-down kingdom."[5]

No wonder some are so mixed up about religion! They hear someone say that Christians are meant to be happy always, but they are not always happy. They hear that Christians are meant to be fulfilled all the time, but sometimes they are not fulfilled. They hear that if they have enough faith, all of their troubles and sicknesses will disappear. Yet, at times they are sick or in trouble.

If we accept self-centered definitions of Christianity and it fails to deliver, the conclusion *must* be that we are not Christian. The other side of this approach is that it is doubtful anyone would refuse a religion that promises gratification for every need, want and desire.

How could an intelligent person say "no" to a faith built on becoming healthy, wealthy and wise just through simply believing? How could anyone resist a religion that promises you will always be protected from the tragedies of nature and even the so-called acts of God?

I cannot imagine anyone unwilling to serve God on those terms—healing every time they are sick and deliverance every time they are in trouble. Even if one were not inclined to be very religious, that proposition would be the pragmatic way to go.

That is, *if it only worked!*

THE PILGRIM'S MOTIVE

Sooner or later we have to deal with this matter of motive. Why do we do what we do? What would it take for God to get us to do more? Or, for Satan to get us to do less? What are the "hot buttons" that motivate us to persevere? What motivations cause us to withdraw, to sulk or to retreat?

Job survived what Satan unleashed, for one reason: his motives for serving God were pure. He did not serve God for what he could get out of it personally, but because he both loved and feared God. Like Job, Paul sought to please God, not himself:

> So we make it our goal to please him, whether we are at home in the body or away from it. For we must all appear before the judgment seat of Christ, that each one may receive what is due him for the things done while in the body, whether good or bad.
>
> Since, then, we know what it is to fear the Lord, we try to persuade men. What we are is plain to God, and I hope it is also plain to your conscience. We are not trying to commend ourselves to you again, but are giving you an opportunity to take pride in us, so that you can answer those who take pride in what is seen rather than in what is in the heart. If we are out of our mind, it is for the sake of God; if we are in our right mind, it is for you. For Christ's love compels us, because we are convinced that one died for all, and therefore all died.
>
> We are therefore Christ's ambassadors, as though God were making his appeal through us.

We implore you on Christ's behalf: Be reconciled to God (2 Corinthians 5:9-14, 20, *NIV*).

PERSONAL EXPERIENCE

The church has a message for lost souls on parade. It is a timeless message of God's love and concern, and it has to be personalized.

Every born-again believer has the message of redemption and grace wrapped up in his or her heart. Each has a testimony of how God came personally to perform the miracle, and of how He stays resident in the heart through the Holy Spirit to give strength and victory every step of life's way.

Lost souls need to hear this testimony. Hearing, they too will find the Way, and will walk in it with a story of their own to tell. In *Secularist Heresy: The erosion of the Gospel in the Twentieth Century*, Harry Blamires reminds us of the danger in trying to market faith through worldly methods:

> We must not exploit our faith by advertising it as a technique for achieving earthly satisfactions. The Faith is not a recipe and not a program. It is a Way. Recipes and programs are made to help you carry out earthly jobs successfully. But a way is something you walk in.[6]

Personal testimony, the one-on-one telling of the story of what God has done in the heart, remains the most powerful tool of evangelism the church has been given. How can we forget so easily? We become wrapped up in the culture and see it as a necessary addition to our message of the Way.

Without question, the manufacturing of religion for the irreligious has become big business. There is a growing abundance of those who offer facsimiles of Christianity. They offer a "more up-to-date" job of providing people what they are looking for. They portray a Christianity without God, one that is more political and philosophical than theological.

These gurus of manufactured religions present themselves as teachers of great mysteries. Know, however, that they are not. They are as the Bible characterizes them, merely false prophets who have risen up to deceive many (see Matthew 24:11).

Their unnatural, frantic work in the name of God is a coverup for a personal lack of devotion to God and a passion for hurting people.

Many believers are tired. They have attended seminars without end. They have been about the busyness of the church for so long they are exasperated. Matters of faith, dogma and conviction have been laid aside in order to get to "important matters" such as growth, buildings, finances and worldly success.

ALTERNATIVE CHOICES

Many Christians are facing today a crisis of faith for the first time in their lives. Faith crises have always occurred; they are not unusual. But it is doubtful any generation has faced one more acute than ours.

We have witnessed some tragic personal failures in many whom we trusted. We placed such a high level of confidence in them that we now feel betrayed. We are challenged to assess our faith through different lenses . . . and many of these views are distorted. We are asked to march to the drumbeat of a pragmatic Christianity that bears little resemblance to the New Testament church.

The major question is this: Are we willing to do God's will out of love alone, or do we do God's will only out of self-interest and only because of what He can do for us? Remember Satan's accusation of Job before the throne of God?

> "Does Job fear God for nothing?" Satan replied. "Have you not put a hedge around him and his household and everything he has? You have blessed the work of his hands, so that his flocks and herds are spread throughout the land. But stretch out your hand and strike everything he has, and he will surely curse you to your face" (Job 1:9-11, _NIV_).

Satan was too shrewd to endeavor to pick holes in Job's conduct, as his friends did later. Satan knew Job was a good man. He knew that this man's reputation would stand extreme scrutiny. Satan also knew that the true character of behavior is determined by motives.

Did Job serve God just for blessings and protection? Or did he serve God out of love? Did Job serve God because of what he expected to gain in this world or the one to come. Or did he serve Him because of who God is?

It is an accepted fact that we live in a period of religious unrest. Yet, in the midst of the unrest there is a cry for real faith. Unfortunately, instead of responding to this cry, institutionalized churches have sent parishioners scurrying for alternatives.

There is no shortage of alternatives! In earshot of the cry for *genuine faith*, numerous churches have resorted to a *glib faith*, or a mere entertainment for attracting the crowds. It is true that pop religion and entertainment bring lots of people to church. It's also true that funerals do the same thing.

GENUINE CHRISTIANITY

We do no favors to anyone by tricking people into believing that Christianity always provides a ready supply of what you need at the moment you need it. This is a pathetic substitute for what Christianity truly offers: a personal relationship with the sovereign God through faith in Jesus Christ, and an eternity with God when this life has ended.

Jesus doesn't want hero worship, He wants divine worship. Jesus asked people to follow Him, not applaud Him. In John 6 He rejected the same worldly acclaim previously offered by the devil in Matthew 4.

Jesus refused to feed the multitude (see John 6:28-35), not because it was wrong to feed hungry people—He had done that before. He had come to *save* them, not to establish a seafood franchise.

He talked about how God's covenant people had been fed manna in the wilderness. He announced Himself now to be both provider and the incarnate provision for their life. If they merely came to Him for the product, they would never understand the fullness of His offering.

In this story the disciples are like church marketers who assume that ministry is motivated either by what those doing the ministry want or by what those being ministered to need. But what about what God desires?

Our culture seems to know more about talking heads than living epistles. Maybe this is why so many Christians have adopted the world's marketing strategy in an attempt to spread the gospel.

Across the recognized divisions of the first century, Christians were a community that refused to be classified or categorized. They simply did not fit. You could find them in the palaces of the wealthy or in the ghettos of the downtrodden. They were from many ethnic origins and represented an assortment of philosophical and educational backgrounds.

There was one thing they had in common, however. They knew they were being guided by a worldview that made them alien to their environment. They knew they were not permanent residents of this earth. Early Christians understood that they were sojourners and strangers.

They were pioneers, not settlers. They were pilgrims, not paraders. They knew that they were just passing through, and that this world was not their home. Reflecting this pilgrim feeling, people in the early days of our church denomination sang such gospel favorites as these:

- "Looking for a City"

- "I Feel Like Traveling On"

- "Marching to Zion"

- "I Can't Feel at Home in This World"

- "I'm Bound for That City"

- "Keep Walking"

- "I'm Too Near Home"

FAITHFUL PILGRIMS

The Bible tells us of the early heroes of faith:

> These all died in faith, not having received the promises, but having seen them afar off were assured of them, embraced them and confessed that they were strangers and pilgrims on the earth. For those who say such things declare plainly that they seek a homeland. And truly if they had called to mind that country from which they had come out, they would have had opportunity to return. But now they desire a better, that is, a heavenly country. Therefore God is not ashamed to be called their God, for He has prepared a city for them (Hebrews 11:13-16).

Although in the world, these early believers expected nothing from it or from its people. They chose not to engage in the affairs of this world, and openly sought another country.

They had no desire to return to where they had come from, and knew that God had provided something better for them. They recognized themselves as strangers and pilgrims on the earth. They determined that they would not allow their passage to be impeded by giving in to the wickedness and the lusts of the lands through which they passed.

LIVING WITNESSES

We keep in mind that we exist as the people of God by gift. We must also remember that we live the Christian life, in a certain sense, by memory. We live through the remembered witness of the saints. Their memories are precious *to us*, and this helps make true Christian living possible *for us*.

Neil Howe and William Strauss say it well:

> There's a revolution underway among today's kids—a *good news* revelation. This generation is going to rebel by behaving not worse, but better. Their life mission will not be to tear down old institutions that don't work, but to build up new ones that do.[7]

Ernest Wright has written succinctly, "The realism of the Bible consists in its close attention to the facts of history. . . . These facts are the facts of God."

Recent articles on evangelicals and their history have hinted that the church is losing its impact on this generation. God help us! As we search our souls, we must ask ourselves some pertinent questions.

Could it be that our experience with God is so lacking that we have lost even the capacity to know what we are missing? Often we talk about the secularization of the culture, but our primary concern should be the increasing secularization of the church.

We must never commit the sin Geoffrey Chaucer did in writing *The Canterbury Tales*—a sin for which he later repented. In this epic story, he described a religious pilgrimage—the annual pilgrimage to Canterbury Cathedral—that turned into a carnival world of popular life in his day.

Chaucer peopled the classic with buffoons and grotesque individuals who committed every type of sin and irreverence imaginable. At the end of the "Parson's Tale," the author asks all who hear or read "this litel trettys" (this little treatise) to pray that Christ would have mercy on him because of his translations and compositions of "worldly vanities."

Our Christian pilgrimage is not a parade or a carnival. We must guard against letting it become either. Our only real chance to win this generation is through a living witness, a vibrant story of personal relationship with the Master. If we lose that, we have lost the key that lets us get into the neighbors' hearts.

When Christian was leaving the City of Destruction to go toward the Celestial City in John Bunyan's *The Pilgrim's Progress*, Evangelist urged Christian to turn a deaf ear to those who hinder him or entice him to turn back:

> Do you see yonder shining light? Keep that light in your eye, and go up directly thereto: so shalt thou see the gate; at which, when thou knockest, it shall be told thee what thou shalt do.

We must keep the light of the Heavenly City in view as we faithfully tell our story to this generation.

Because the Word of God has been preserved and delivered to us in a language and format we can understand, we are able to read the story for our story for ourselves and know the truthfulness of it.

Along our own personal life's journey we are stopped by historical markers and prompted to utter thanks for those who paid a great price to bring us the gospel. They worked hard and long to keep the church doors open, to keep the Sunday school going, to witness to us of God's great and mighty acts.

Now, it is up to us to pass along both *the story* and *our story* to another generation.

We are not on parade; we are on a lifelong pilgrimage. We have a task to perform and a story to tell. As His *living epistles,* we are to be read of all.

CHAPTER

2

Being a
People of
Covenant

You shall receive power when the Holy Spirit has come upon you; and you shall be witnesses to Me. . . .

(Acts 1:8)

*W*hat does it mean for us to be a people of covenant? When Christ came, He boldly announced the kingdom of God. He proclaimed to the world the peace and well-being God wishes for all people.

Now both Jew and Gentile alike have access in the Spirit to God the Father through Jesus Christ. Gentiles are no longer strangers and aliens but full citizens with all the saints. We are members of the household of God, joint-heirs with Christ and brothers and sisters to one another.

This new covenant is built on the foundation of the apostolic testimony in the prophetic announcement of the fulfillment of the promise. The Messiah has come. The Spirit has been poured out. The end has begun. The kingdom of heaven is at hand!

Jesus is the cornerstone of the entire spiritual structure. As living stones we are growing into a holy temple in the Lord where He dwells, just as we dwell in His presence.

We are written into God's story through the new covenant, a fulfillment of the old. This means that God has written His will in our minds, hearts, understanding and desires. We have a common testimony, and we are to live in a corporate process of formation for our own good and for the good of the whole world!

Stephen indicated in Acts 7 that we are a church in the wilderness on a pilgrimage through the world. We are commissioned to proclaim truth, and to love our neighbors in the power and demonstration of the Holy Spirit. We are His people! Today the issue is, Shall we *have* church or *be* the church? Which is primary?

CONTEMPORARY PATTERNS

Clearly, we must understand that being a Christian means being a part of Christ's body, the church. Suppose my children came to my wife and me tonight and asked, "What is for supper?" "Why do you ask?" we would say. "Well, we have been taking a survey of various homes in the community in order to determine where we would like to eat supper tonight."

My wife and I would reply that we are a family, not a collection of individuals. The point is not to determine what we might prefer individually. Rather, it is to have a family meal. We *are* a family; therefore we share a common meal.

This is the problem with the church today. Although we have a corporate covenant, we find ourselves shopping for the ecclesiastical franchise of our choice. Rather than using the traditional images, let me suggest some contemporary models which feel more like church in North America.

CIRCUS CHURCHES

Some churches feel like a circus. You know the type: the pastor is a ringmaster who books various acts because he knows they are crowd pleasers. The people enjoy chills and thrills, and are entertained by seeing others take risks. People pay money for a ticket and sit enthralled while the music plays and the acts are introduced one by one.

Perhaps it is even on television! I actually heard of a church where a 7-foot man skydived out of an airplane into a parking lot to begin a revival service. He billed himself as Goliath, and he always seemed to draw a large crowd.

What could be wrong with this method, some ask, _as long as people get saved? After all, are we not to save some "by all means"?_

Actually, what is wrong is that this kind of behavior always trivializes the glorious gospel of the Cross and the resurrection message of Jesus Christ. Indeed, we have no trouble at all imagining what the Christ of John 6 would say: "Unless you eat My body and drink My blood, you cannot be My disciple" (see v. 53).

FILLING STATION CHURCHES

What about the church as a "filling station"? The purpose of the church, in this example, is to pump blessings to as many people as possible.

The pastor's role in it all is that of a station manager who hires various specialists (lining up specialized ministries?) who, in turn, perform special services for the customers.

The people are never involved in service to each other; this is what they pay others to do. In this situation believers have no common ministry, except to tell others where they themselves get serviced. They get just enough blessings to keep them on their daily tasks.

When they run low or near empty, they drive back to the station for a new filling. When the station down the street pumps the same blessing for a cheaper price, this is where they go, even if it causes the engine to knock a bit.

Private Club Churches

The third example of contemporary churches is that of a private club. The pastor or owner books various people who entertain as comedians, singers or magicians. These headliners draw a crowd and help create a regular clientele to pay the bills for the club. If the club comes up with an exciting enough formula, then perhaps it can be franchised in other cities.

In these examples, people have no accountability or responsibility to one another. Their "needs" are met, but their needs are not turned into service to their neighbor. They are not asked to sacrifice. They are never told that to find their lives they must lose them. Their joy is superficial. They never have a deep-felt lament in the face of the pain and disappointment of modern life.

The only concern the managers have is how many are served, how much money is taken in, how often and what services are provided at what profit margin. Unfortunately, the church seems to take many of its cues from the therapeutic culture of our consumer society. Leaders of the church are held to one criterion—do they know how to manage well.

People may share or disclose their stories to others, but there is no deep sharing in the *lives* of one another. They do not obey the Scriptural injunction to bear one another's burdens. They listen to each other's stories as people watch television and listen to Oprah, Jerry Springer and a host of other media talking heads. The leaders build a good clientele but not a community.

This therapeutic culture seeks to release people from guilt, to alleviate their pain and to give them a good time in general, but no one is asked to share in the healing/salvation ministry of Jesus. Or to become a wounded healer who is touched and moved with the feelings and infirmities of others.

No one's pain is deepened until it makes her or him able to minister to others who have been deeply wounded, defiled and offended.

People are freed up from everything, including responsibility, but they are not bound back together in the deep, organic bonds of the body of Jesus Christ. Instead of becoming an end-time missionary fellowship, they become faces in the crowd, virtually unknown by and to others—even in small groups.

BIBLICAL PATTERNS

Think, on the other hand, of how the Bible envisions the church in vivid images of redemptive grace.

The Body of Christ

The church is the body of Christ. This means that each member is organically related to the others. For this reason, one part of the body cannot say to another, "I don't need you." If one part of the body hurts and another part doesn't feel it, then it means that something is wrong. We soon learn that pain is not our greatest enemy and pleasure is not our greatest friend.

A hand surgeon in India spent hours in a complicated operation, and reattached numerous tendons around the wrist of a patient. He sent the patient home only to have him return a few days later. At that point the surgeon had to amputate the hand and part of the arm.

The reason was that the man had gone to sleep on the floor of his home, and rats had come and gnawed through the bandages. Because the man could feel no pain, he never woke up until the next morning. If only he had felt the pain, his arm might have been saved.

How many churches would still be alive and vital if they could only feel the pain of others? Without sharing in the pain, it is impossible to share in the true joy.

A Missionary Fellowship

The church is a missionary fellowship in these last days. There is a feeling of urgency in the body of Christ, but there is also a deep sense of togetherness. Caring believers who share a common mission become comrades-in-arms. Their mission is to love God and neighbors, and to disciple the nations.

This missionary fellowship also takes on a local character as believers pray together about which part of the world God wants them to love, which neighbors to touch and what training and resources are needed to care in a costly way. They focus their faith on leading those about them into the knowledge of Jesus Christ. Then new recruits become a part of this fellowship, too, this pilgrimage on the way to the Kingdom.

This kind of fellowship looks inward, to be sure, but it also has an outward focus and a clear direction toward the kingdom of God. A fellowship that is only turned outward burns out from sheer activism. If it only turns inward, it soon degenerates into a selfish "bless me club" which never really takes on trouble by attacking the strongholds of Satan and freeing the captives. The church must look both inward and outward.

THE PEOPLE OF GOD

The church, the people of God, is the only people in the world with a story that encompasses the whole universe and everyone in it. It is the only people without a national constitution, an exclusive racial ideology, a social class exclusiveness, or some required level of education or income.

What tremendous political implications! The Day of Pentecost was a political event. God poured out His Spirit on His people that believers may be a house of prayer for the healing of all nations.

To be a people of God is to share in the sole covenant of life. God intended this from the beginning. It is what Jesus came to fulfill when He said, "I have come that they may have life, and that they may have it more abundantly" (John 10:10).

When Israel was no people, God made them His people by leading them out of bitter bondage in Egypt. He led them through the wilderness, into the Promised Land. He gave them victory over their enemies so they could be a light to the nations. Even when they were unfaithful, God was faithful.

John the Baptist called all Israel out to the desert. He "turned them out of the church" and invited them back into repentance because the kingdom of heaven was, and is, at hand. He was preparing the way for Jesus the Messiah.

COVENANT PATTERNS

Jesus commissioned this new people He called—both Jew and Gentile alike—to go into all the world and make disciples of all nations (Matthew 28:19, 20).

Did God's plan change from calling a covenant people with a corporate existence to calling individuals who would experience only personal salvation? No! It did not. It was God's intention to have a covenant people—those who would live in the new covenant in the blood of Jesus Christ. We must understand the difference between living in covenant relationship and a contract.

COVENANT AND CONTRACT

Both *covenant* and *contract* envision relational bonds, but contract relationships are based on and directed by mutual self-interest. Covenant bonds are based on and directed by a common, ultimate commitment to God according to the Scriptures. A *marriage contract* may be a 50-50 operation, but a *marriage covenant* is a 100 percent concern.

A *marriage contract* represents two people making a social agreement with legal recognition, but a *marriage covenant* involves God and the people of God. There is a commitment in a marriage covenant to image the love of the triune God in human community at its basic level—the family.

A contract bond understands the value of other persons only in terms of their instrumental value "for me." In a covenant the value of other persons is derived not from the instrumental worth "for me," but from the same spiritual source that gives meaning to my life.

In a contract with someone to build a house, a person has value as the builder of the house—this is instrumental value. This person is "my" builder and thus of value to me.

In a holy covenant, other people receive value from the same source we do. Every person is made in the image of God and is of infinite worth. Christ died for all. He does not want anyone to perish, but He wants all to come to repentance.

COVENANT AND COMPETITION

In a contract, each party gives as little as possible

in order to receive as much as possible. Fierce nego-tiating usually surrounds a contract. But in a cov-enant relationship, true bonding is experienced the moment one party relates to the other out of a deep, authentic commitment to God. In this relationship of love, there is no calculation; there is only extrava-gant self-giving.

In a contract relationship, self-interest and self-sufficiency are the norms for getting one's needs met. Within a holy covenant, we are bound together by becoming the servants of one another. We wash each other's feet. We take the risk of depending on another for receiving the gifts and graces of God.

In a contract, we may consider people so weak that we must always take care of them, or so strong we must always control them. But in a covenant, relationships are open and dynamic. The future will be better than the past or the present because we are on a journey toward God together.

Covenant and Critical Concerns

The implications for the church are clear. The contract church, based on and directed by mutual self-interest, values other persons only in terms of their worth "for me." What can I get out of this? What needs do I have to be met?

Each person then calculates giving as little as possible in order to get as much as possible from the church. Church becomes something we "have" in the same way that we have a pizza!

Strategy for the contract church appeals to people's

self-interest and their need for self-sufficiency, rather than emphasizing the believers' interdependence.

People in the contract church don't want to be bothered with the weak. The strong, though they may be praised and honored, are not to be imitated or to become examples for us or for our young.

We of the new covenant in the blood of Jesus share, however, a common testimony. We testify that God has graciously called us out of the world and placed us in the covenant bonds of His people. Each person thus called and redeemed, becomes my brother, my sister, my mother, my father and my children in the family of faith.

Each person is of infinite value. The church becomes home for the strong, the weak, the carnal and the spiritual, all in the process of becoming what God wants them to be. To sin against someone in such a covenant bond is to sin against the image of God and, therefore, to sin against God himself. He has placed His name upon these believers.

To serve one another and God and to be served by others and by God is what the covenant entails, because the Son of Man came not to be served but to serve.

We receive the ministry of others to ourselves because God has distributed gifts according to the measure of faith given to each in the body. In covenant, people learn to depend on one another, to bear one another's burdens, and to enable one another to bear his or her own burdens.

There is a divine strengthening and empowering

in the covenant church. This enables others to be welcomed into the fellowship and cared for just as we have been.

Our Patterns

The covenant church looks beyond the present exchange of goods and services and meeting of immediate needs to the future together in the kingdom of God. In the early years of the latter-day Pentecostal revival, people thought of themselves as being part of a Pentecostal *movement*. There wasn't much talk of being part of an institution or a denomination.

In this movement people had a definite sense of identity that was distinct from that of the world around them. They burned their bridges to the past with its old friends and old desires.

Remembering the Story

People in the movement believed that they were a part of a last-days move of God to prepare the church for the coming of Christ and to gather the nations into His body. Though every member was not an evangelist, everyone was a witness.

Early Pentecostals had organization, but it was looser and more flexible than it is now. Several people would take the leadership over this or that ministry in reaching out to others and in caring for people in need. Recruitment was face-to-face, and opposition only made the movement grow, as men and women came to depend on God and on one another more.

In this setting, a typical Church of God testimony

emerged. Perhaps you remember it as I do:

> I thank the Lord that I am saved, sanctified and filled with the Holy Ghost; and a member of the great Church of God; and on my way to heaven. Pray for me that I will hold out faithfully to the end.

Having publicly affirmed their lives in terms of this Pentecostal paradigm of faith development, individuals would go on to review the events of the past week in the light of the meaning given by their testimony.

It was a shared journey and a shared testimony. In the community of believers there would be praises and prayer requests. There would be tears and laughter. Usually the service would end in a corporate prayer, each for the others.

MEANING IN THE STORY

Notice what this triumphant testimony entailed. Many would testify they had been called out of darkness. They had been called into the light and had made a radical break with the world. *Thus they were "saved."*

Further, they testified that they had put off everything that they thought might be unlike Christ. This included bad habits, bad language, bad associations, and things that were clearly prohibited by Scripture. They had rid themselves, with God's help, of things that did not represent the highest commitment to holiness.

They testified that they had "prayed through" about

this, and were yielded to God. Many said they would go where God wanted them to go and do and be what He wanted them to do and be.

With the vessel having thus been prepared, *the Holy Ghost had come to fill each one, and they shared in the joy of this experience.* It had given them a new sense of courage, and brought with it other gifts of the Spirit that empowered them and gave them greater confidence in God.

To be a member of the Church of God was a good thing, they felt and testified. Some understood this in an exclusive sense. While most opposed this exclusiveness, there was still a rightful sense of pride in being a member of a church whose standard of living was holiness.

All of them were convinced that they were on their way to heaven, and they sang about it often. They would literally pray and sing heaven down into their souls as they rejoiced in their common destiny.

There was always a recognition that one would be tested, however. Thus they emphasized the request, *"Pray for me that I will hold out faithfully to the end."*

NEGLECTING THE STORY

Today, much of this testimony is gone. What happened? Part of the problem lies in the failure to understand each of these experiences as having ongoing significance in the life of the Christian. "Saved," "sanctified" and "filled" all seemed to be in the past tense. That left only the newness of miracles and the spectacular manifestation of gifts to keep the wonder alive.

Church commitments, meant to guide people into holiness, became reasons for excluding others. Often, teachings that began as matters of cultivation in holiness became tests of fellowship.

An intense desire for Biblical holiness, while present, sometimes degenerated into legalism that no longer contained the passion of God and humility of spirit which were intended to be its beauty.

Upward mobility meant that more people could afford things that had been prohibited in times past. This, and a reaction to legalism, meant that more money and effort could now be invested in bigger houses, bigger cars, jewelry and other non-necessities of life.

Third-, fourth-, and fifth-generation children grew up in the church. By living in a "religious cocoon," they had not known a radical break with the world. Many could not remember the specific time they were saved. Parents eager to protect their children from the legalism of the past were often afraid to impose any discipline and discipleship for fear their young would misunderstand grace.

Where are we now? Some Pentecostals are no more than excited evangelicals who have lost the militant missionary edge and their passion for the holy God. Their personal commitment to mortify the deeds of the flesh has become a desire to grow only gradually.

Bewildered middle-aged adults are glad the

church has overcome legalism, but are not quite sure what to do about the new liberty of many of their brothers and sisters in the church.

In some churches, social drinking, profanity, going to questionable movies (or renting the videos!), dressing immodestly, and going after the glitz and glamour of the world have become the order of the day. Many people are uneasy and restless with these trends.

They remember the battles of yesterday and, with some young adults who don't, pray for a genuine renewing in the Holy Spirit that will lead to a deepened passion for God as well as for men and women in society.

This picture emerges too often in North America. While the church grows like wildfire outside the United States, inside there are too many classes of Christians who have plateaued or are declining.

RENEWAL PATTERNS

Thank God, however, there are signs of hope everywhere. Individuals and churches are busy seeking to recover an authentic Pentecostal testimony so that Pentecostalism will not become "Pentecostal-was-ism" (a word/phrase coined by Dr. Rickie Moore, my colleague at the Church of God Theological Seminary).

As He did in Israel, God is raising up prophets and prophetesses who are radical conservatives. They remind the church of the roots of its covenant with God. It is still radical to speak of a church that understands every Christian is to be a Christ-like witness in the power of the Holy Spirit.

As we hear again the radical claims of the holy God, we are driven to repentance and are borne along by God and His gracious love daily. This is what grace is—God's love working mercifully in all of us and for all of us. Life becomes a wonderful gift to those who are newly sensitized to the culture of death around us and are no longer willing to dance to its rhythms.

THE STORY AND SANCTIFICATION

Men and women are rediscovering sanctification. They are learning anew about a wholehearted devotion to God with no known holdouts or resistance to Him. Sanctification is an integration of the heart in which one is utterly sincere and open to all the admonitions, exhortations, corrections and instructions of Scripture. More than a onetime experience, it is a daily abiding in the love of God.

People are discovering that there is still something to praying through when resistance and evil desires arise. They are learning to mortify the deeds of the flesh, and not simply to grow by telling a few less lies and lusting a little less. Sanctification means that God fixes our "want to" where some Christians are so unstable (double-minded).

Others pray and confess, and are searched by the Spirit through the Word until the blood of Christ cleanses them from all filthiness of flesh and spirit (2 Corinthians 7:1). Thus filled with the love of God, these people find it impossible not to care for their neighbors in a costly way.

The love of God in this world always means compassion, and compassion is the magnificent motive. Those filled with His love seek to care as Jesus cares for those about them. They feed them, clothe them, visit them in prison, and see them delivered from demonic oppression and possession. They encourage the disenfranchised and see them empowered by the Lord to be more than victims.

THE STORY AND THE SPIRIT

As you and I do these things, we encounter the strongholds of Satan and see once again our need for the power of the Holy Spirit. The desire to be filled with the Spirit while not desiring to be a witness is an ugly thing indeed. Is anything more horrendous and contradictory than a Pentecostal church that is not involved in costly witness and mission?

People filled with the Spirit learn the meaning of praying without ceasing (see 1 Thessalonians 5:17). They learn to pray according to the will of God because they are instructed in the Scriptures. They pray with sighs too deep for words because the love of God constrains them and draws them to their neighbors in need.

They pray with the Spirit and speak in tongues. This means that they are engaged cognitively, affectively and spiritually in responding to God and to the world about them. Prayer becomes a way of life. Walking in the Spirit and walking in prayer are integral parts of this way of life.

The renewal of our covenant with God means that we live in radical gratitude because we know that except for the grace of God, we too would be floundering. This gratitude becomes a foundation for our witness in mission. It means that we will love until it hurts.

This compassion draws us out of ourselves to others. It means we are emboldened as we pray with our spirits, in the Holy Spirit, and are given courage to stand against the forces of accusation and death. We will be more Christ-conscious than self-conscious.

THE STORY AND PERSONAL VICTORY

The dynamic of the Spirit drives us into the world with courage and boldness to care as God cares and love as He loves. To be filled with the Spirit will also fill us with God's care.

This does not mean keeping one's head down, trying to make it anonymously into heaven; it means standing up and being counted. It means finding the front lines of the mission or church in your area, and standing shoulder to shoulder with other soldiers of the Cross.

To change the metaphor, it means that we are not sailing on a love boat with games and drinking and parading around in various stages of undress in order to hook up with someone. Instead, we are on a battleship. We are shipmates.

During a war people still love and marry and get educated and work, but everything is understood in light of the war effort. Everything they do or that happens to them is understood in light of the desired victory.

We will not attend the church of our choice if we recover our covenant. Rather, we will be stationed and deployed by God. We will open our hearts and our homes to others so that we can tell the story of God's blessing, discipline and leading in our own lives.

We will tell honest stories about our own struggles with God and with ourselves. We will see our neighborhoods and cities in God's light. We will walk the streets together, asking God to give us mission eyes.

Our worship services will move away from trying to orchestrate a TV production to the recovery of worship as the work of the whole people of God. Choruses and hymns that tell the story of redemption will reemerge. Worship will no longer be the performance of the pastor backed by the choir.

To be sure, the pastor will lead in worship, but his or her leadership will maximize the participation of all the people of God. Pastoral prayers and the intercessory prayers of the people will include praise and lament, joy and longing.

There will be a place to hear the testimonies of the people of God. Young people will hear the stories of the old. They will understand the ethical challenges of the day in the light of the passion for God in the lives of those who have proven faithful over the decades.

Older people will be encouraged as they hear the passion and see the witness of the young. The middle-aged will mentor others, and pass on the faith to their children, to new converts and to their neighbors. Then it will no longer be bad, questionable or rare for someone to seek God without having been called into a ministry. When we understand ourselves in a missionary situation, we will pray for the Lord of the harvest to send many laborers into the harvest.

If we are to reclaim our testimony, we must understand that it will be found among the poor, the needy, the bound and the disenfranchised. Concern and genuine love for these people will overcome our strategies of affluence and safety. These kinds of ministries will tax our hoarded resources, both financially and spiritually.

To go into the dark places, we will need the light of the Word more than ever. If we go into the places of hate and impurity, we will need the holiness and love of God more than ever. If we go into the places of spiritual wickedness and evil beasts, we will need the power of the Holy Spirit and His authority more than ever.

In such an environment, care receivers will become care givers who empower others with righteous love and God's power. We will multiply churches that grow by face-to-face, hand-to-hand witnessing, the tearing down of great strongholds, and by careful, patient love. We are the people of God in a covenant of care with Him and with people.

CHAPTER

3

GETTING THE STORY STRAIGHT

And they overcame [the devil] by the blood of the Lamb and by the word of their testimony, and they did not love their lives to the death (Revelation 12:11).

*U*nlike the stories that claim to give the meaning of life for a particular person, the Christian story claims to give the meaning of human life in general. While the Christian story is a collection of stories, all of them combined present a particular narrative.

In this chapter we will consider all human existence as narrative. We will look at the Jewish view of history, the story of Jesus, our story in light of these stories, and what it means to be on the Way with Christ in our daily lives.

THE STORY AND NARRATIVE EXISTENCE

Our existence is a narrative existence. To remain on the straight and narrow way in the Christian life, we have to get, and keep, the story of Jesus straight so that we can discern what is consistent and what is contradictory about it. It is said that history is *His story*. We must remember this truth in the midst of the conflicting stories around us in the world.

Through the centuries, men and women have given their lives because they interpreted them in the light of the history of the people of God, and His revelation in that history. Whatever story we tell about our family, nation, race or political affiliation—they all have to be told in the light of the Biblical story if we are faithful Christians.

Human existence has a narrative quality. Every human being lives between memory and hope. We cannot know who we are without memory. Someone tells us stories about our family, about our parents, about where we have come from and what we are about. From these stories we gain a sense of our identity.

We are also persons who live in hope. We plan. We have certain expectations. We have a certain vision of the future. Between memory and hope we begin to construct the meaning of who we are.

All human existence has a "know-be-do" character. That is, every human raises the questions: "How can I truly know who I am and what life is about? Who will tell me the truth about this?"

After you hear the stories from your parents and other trusted persons, you have to decide for yourself at some point what is true and authentic human existence. You have to sort through the various stories you hear and decide by which story you will finally live.

Every human raises the question of being, not in the general, philosophical sense, but in a personal sense. Each person asks, "Who shall I be?" Each person wonders what character traits to cultivate in himself or herself and in the children or friends entrusted to the person for discipling. Each individual also asks how he or she should live.

Once you receive stories about what life is in general, and what your life is about in particular, you have to decide what is consistent with your stories about life, meaning and value.

Knowing who we are can be a real problem in

today's world. Who will tell us the truth? How can we avoid self-deception? So many of us grow up learning to please others. We learn early to project the kind of image and say the words that bring approval from those around us.

We are in many different contexts in any given day or week, however. We are with different people who have different expectations of us. The problem is that we can end up acting differently in each situation. We are prone to project to others what we think they want. But at the end of the day when we are alone in our beds, the question remains, "Who am I?"

So the problem is compounded. It is not just a question of which stories about our lives are true, but is our self-report true? Every human comes to realize that every exercise of freedom carries with it a destiny or a consequence. A person can choose to jump off the top of a house on his head, but then he will have to live with the consequences. (In this instance he may not live very long!)

Choices made about who we are, what characters we develop and honor, what is right and wrong, and what is the source of true knowledge begin to shape and determine the kind of person we are.

Is it any wonder, then, that so many people live in cynicism, despair or boredom? This is especially true in a culture of radical relativism where people are told that there is no true story; or even if there is one, you can't know it with certainty.

When people despair of real meaning, they turn

to living for the moment. They cease to be agents of a larger historical drama and seek to reproduce pleasurable experiences that will medicate the pain in their lives.They may turn to drugs, alcohol, illicit sex or constant partying.This is an act of desperation, whether it is done quietly or frantically.

This truth applies to many Christians who, though they may have heard the Christian story, do not really live out that story. The Scriptural view of history does not direct their life decisions about their identity, to whom they belong and what they should do in the world.

Living this way, they adopt abstract principles of truth or good divorced from a real knowledge of, and obedience to, the Scripture. They try to focus only on pleasurable moments and experiences as a way to avoid their own pain and despair. Sometimes people even do this with worship.

If the point of worship is only to have an experience that makes people feel better, then they don't need to know the Biblical story. They don't need to know each other's stories of joy and hope and pain and fear. They don't need to bear each other's burdens. They don't need to intercede. They don't need to lament as well as rejoice.

All they need to do is to preach, sing and pray fast enough and loud enough to reproduce the good feeling they had at the previous service. The problem with this, of course, is that it begins to require greater and greater effort. They must have more spectacular stories or events. They must have more celebrities and better entertainment!

All of life's experiences demand interpretation. Many people suffer from deep-seated disappointment with God, along with personal doubts and creeping boredom. Only the truth of Scripture, constantly remembered and faithfully attended to, can deliver us from a life of episodic relief.

THE STORY AND JEWISH HISTORY

God seeks to make all of us agents of history on mission with Him, rather than victims of passing time and changing circumstances. This hopeful view of history is God's gift to all people through His people, Israel.

In a way we can say that the Jews invented history. The Old Testament people of God experienced pain, joy, sorrow, disappointment, victory and hope. They wrote these experiences in stories as they were moved on by the Holy Spirit.

These stories were widely circulated. They were joined together in the understanding of the people of God to become a worldview. These stories together became one hermeneutical story—that is, a story that interpreted all other stories and gave meaning to Israel's life.

When a new event would occur, whether a painful or a joyful event, God's people would understand that event in the light of the Scriptural story, the revealed truth about God and their life and destiny. This Jewish view of history that comprised the inheritance of the people of God everywhere and at all times had seven characteristics.

1. *History was a developing story.* Its genesis was an integration of stories the Hebrews understood as a part of an unfinished story. God, who had delivered them out of bitter bondage in Egypt and had created them anew and afresh as a distinct people, was the same God who had created all worlds for His glory and pleasure.

God's way with humankind was not finished, however. There would be a day of the Lord.

2. *History was a meaningful story.* All things have a beginning and move toward an end. God, who created all things, had an end or purpose in view when He created this people. This means that nothing created is above God. No creature or historical person can be worshiped. There can be no images to substitute for God.

3. *History was a continuing story.* God caused the beginning and He will accomplish the end He desires. There is no cause greater than God. He not only causes things to begin, God works in all things because of His purpose. This contrasts with the deists' view that God simply began the world and let it run by its own internal principles or laws.

In the Hebrew view, the Creator not only began all things and maintains all things in existence, He also intervenes in history. He lifts up and puts down rulers and kingdoms to judge and deliver, to wound and to heal. This God who is above history also acts in history and sustains everything at every moment.

4. *History was a limited story.* If you have ever felt that your life was simply going in circles, then you have much in common with a lot of ancient men and women. For centuries people believed that history was a cycle like that of the seasons that recur over and over again.

Many people held that the stars or the fates, which they considered to be the rulers in the heavens, were really running things in earth. These gods above would determine destiny on earth. Individuals had to find their places in the cycles and accept their fate.

For the Hebrews, however, history was not a series of circles and cycles. It was a time line. This time line had a beginning and an end, but it had a definite forward movement.

5. *History was a purposeful story.* Within this linear, purposeful view of history every person, event and act was seen as unique and in some way affecting history. God desires each individual to become a free agent who will break free from the bondage and victimization of sin and the rulers of the power of darkness.

God had a purpose for every person, they felt, and was worked through all events to accomplish His purpose for the good of those who loved Him. Of course, this also meant that evil people were given a measure of freedom. They could exercise their will by killing and oppressing others. They could reject God's purpose, create their own and live within the bondage they had chosen.

Would this mean, then, that God's plan and purpose for history was thwarted?

6. *History was a hopeful story.* In spite of the choices of evil people or the activity of evil forces, this Scriptural view of history holds that God keeps His promises. Therefore, this view of history became a covenant-missionary history. God made a covenant of life with His people in the midst of the cultures of death in the world. He was a missionary God who freed men and women to join Him in making history and living purposeful lives.

To know God was to be in history with a people. It was to live in covenant love—God's steadfast love. Salvation was a journey from darkness and bondage to light and freedom. Salvation was following God and walking in the path of His precepts. Abraham was typical. Open to God's future, he heard the voice of God and left the known and fixed to begin a journey into the unknown.

7. *History was a memorial story.* For the Hebrews, worship became a way of faithfully remembering. The various pieces of the Biblical story were put together in the same way detached members of the body might be reattached surgically.

The Hebrews were invited to always remember that they were slaves in Egypt and wandering Aramaeans whom God called out to fulfill His covenant purposes. This remembering became a way to perceive all of reality, as they faithfully remembered the stories in their worship.

They were not only remembering history, they were reenacting it. They were gathering a people from all people. God had called them to be a light to the nations. Through them God had determined to give His gifts of law and life and liberty. He had committed to them the oracles of God!

THE TEMPLE

Jewish worship in the first century A.D. occurred in three locations: the Temple, the synagogue and the family home.

In the Temple, the historical celebrations of Israel's deliverance and blessing were remembered with the cycles of planting and harvesting throughout the year. On designated occasions trumpets were blown, sacrifices were made, the incense was burned, and the great day of Atonement was remembered.

THE SYNAGOGUE

In the synagogue, those who were dispersed among the nations gathered to hear the reading of the Scripture, to sing and to pray. Far removed from the Temple at Jerusalem, they nevertheless sought to be faithful in hearing the Word of God in the synagogues, and applying it to their daily lives.

THE FAMILY

In the family, the central act of worship that was meant to secure personal identity and belonging was the

Passover meal (called the *Seder*). Every aspect of this meal was meant to remind each participant of his or her deliverance from the bondage in Egypt, and of God's preservation of His people in the wilderness as He brought them into the Promised Land.

Other meals related to the Passover meal. One of these was the *Chaburah*. This meal was sponsored by a Hebrew institution, like a burial or ancestor society. Someone who had been an especially faithful witness in living out the covenant with God was honored and remembered at the rite/meal.

Bread was broken, a cup was lifted, a meal shared, then a final cup of blessing would end the Chaburah celebration.

Another significant meal in the life of the Jewish believer was the *Kiddush*. This meal ushered in and sanctified the Sabbath Day celebration. Prayer over the bread ended with a cup of blessing and a further prayer: "Blessed be the Lord God who brings forth bread from wheat as thou brought your children forth from Egypt."

The prayer shows how Creation and redemption were joined in the Jewish mind. The Creator God is the Redeemer; the One who provides food provides freedom. As we recall this part of our Biblical heritage, we remember that Jesus was a Jew.

The Story and Jesus' Story

If all the things that happened in Jesus' life were written in books, the world could not contain them

(John 21:25). The writers of the Gospels, moved by the same Holy Spirit who moved on the writers of the Hebrew scriptures, selected and profiled certain facts in telling the story of Jesus. They present their narratives in such a way that all subsequent believers would be saved, instructed and equipped by His story.

As a Jew, Jesus attended the synagogue observances in Nazareth, the Temple observances in Jerusalem. He sat regularly with His family at the Sabbath meal. No doubt He was part of the meals of remembrance (Chaburah), honoring some faithful relative or friend of the family.

Jesus honored the Law, the Torah. He kept the Temple observances and the traditional limits of the Word of God. He asserted that not one jot or tittle of the Law would pass away until all was fulfilled (Matthew 5:18).

He enjoined those cleansed from leprosy to go and show themselves to the priest according to the Law (Mark 1:40-44). He warned His disciples that their righteousness must exceed that of the scribes and Pharisees (Matthew 5:20). At Jesus' transfiguration, Moses and Elijah, representing the Law and the Prophets, were present with Him in glory (see Matthew 17:1-8; Mark 9:2-8; Luke 9:28-36).

Jesus was faithful to the ancient covenant, but He also announced the inbreaking of the coming kingdom of God. He called on all people everywhere to repent in the light of that coming kingdom. He stated, "You have heard it said . . . but I say to you . . ." (see

Matthew 5:21-39). In this way, He was shown to be the Word of God incarnate.

He forgave sins and taught that He was before Abraham (John 8:58). When He said such things as "The Sabbath was made for man, and not man for the Sabbath" (Mark 2:27), He indicated anew and afresh that God's priority was people.

New possibilities of grace shone through as He pronounced to the woman caught in the act of adultery that she should go and sin no more (John 8:11). Her sins were forgiven!

The Law was being fulfilled as Jesus established the new covenant (see Matthew 5:17). In His person, He created a place to meet God and find redemption. This gracious opening fulfilled the Law.

In the deepening covenant of life, Jesus offered Himself in service and sacrifice for the sins of the world. Jews and Gentiles alike are called into the Kingdom—men and women, bond and free, Romans and Jews. Jesus depicted Samaritans as good (see Luke 10:30-37), and a Syro-Phoenician "dog" found a place at the Master's table (see Matthew 15:21-28).

Our Lord Jesus was no victim of history. He freely offered Himself to the Father in the power of the Holy Spirit, so that men and women everywhere could know the truth and live in covenant freedom.

THE STORY AND YOUR STORY

The story of your life is made up of millions of facts and events, and hundreds of persons. As you tell your story, you profile those facts and choose the most significant ones that shaped you to become the person you are.

As you interpret your story in the light of the Christian story and our shared Pentecostal story, you claim a Spirit-filled identity and live it out as a witness before the watching world. As you walk in the light as Jesus is in the light, you have fellowship with others, and His blood keeps on cleansing you from all unrighteousness (see 1 John 1:7).

This means that our Pentecostal spirituality has an oral, or narrative, character. We must testify to one another and to the watching world. It is not just that we have testimony services (though we must have those), it means our lives are to be a testimony. The power of the blood of Jesus and the power of the Holy Spirit enable us to be witnesses to Christ in all the world and in everything we do.

We preach, teach, sing and tell our stories as we continually remember our Biblical heritage and try to be faithful. We raise our children and we receive new members into the church in order to form them in the stories of our faith.

Since our stories are a part of the Christian story, it is important to tell others how the story operates in our lives. We become the illustrated version of the Scriptures, living epistles!

Sermons that lift only abstract principles, songs that simply repeat slogans (Is this vain repetition?), and family devotions that occur without ever sharing our real life stories—all of these can undermine our covenant faithfulness and deny the essentially historical character of our faith.

As we remember and live out the story, our lives are continually being sanctified. The world, the flesh and the devil attempt to shut down the story and make us victims of carnal desires, worldly ideologies and demonic plots. But we have the confident assurance of overcoming power.

The Spirit who inspired the Scripture enabled Jesus to offer Himself on the cross, fell on the disciples at Pentecost and is working in all things. This Spirit fills every sanctified vessel so that we may shine as lights of the world and tell the truth with our lives.

When the Scriptures direct the script of our lives, we are actors who are free to love as God loved. As we tell our stories faithfully in the light of God's story, or the Scriptures, our words will minister grace to each other and invite our neighbors into the family.

If we get the story straight, and as we are taught and led by the Holy Spirit, we will stay on the straight and narrow path to the kingdom of heaven and take many with us!

4
CHAPTER

BECOMING

A

WITNESS

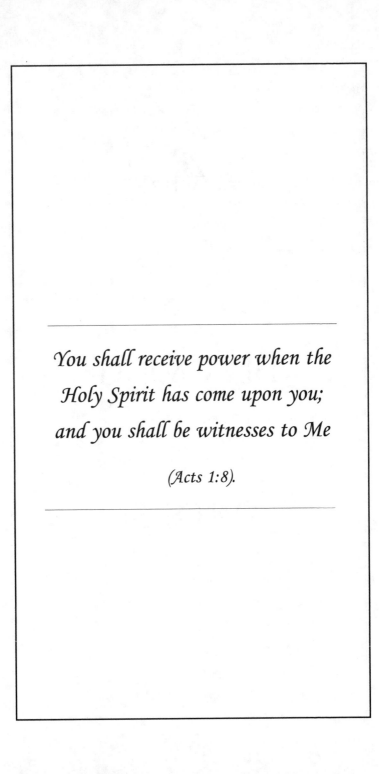

You shall receive power when the Holy Spirit has come upon you; and you shall be witnesses to Me

(Acts 1:8).

When the Holy Spirit pours the love of God into our hearts, trouble usually shows up. With the life-changing Spirit within us, we begin to love God, love the truth, and love people in the world the way God loves them. Those who seek to love God usually suffer persecution, however, when the love of truth is rejected and actively opposed.

Stephen was persecuted in Acts 7 when he tried to tell his countrymen the truth about Jesus Christ. As he reviewed their history in the light of God's revelation, the crowd took up stones to kill him. As he looked into heaven, he saw Jesus at the right hand of the Father (v. 56)!

Becoming a witness is a life-and-death matter. It is about life in the face of death, and about life over against death. It is about triumphing in the midst of a culture of death. God wants us to be total witnesses.

This is more than simply a matter of *giving* a witness. We must *become* witnesses of Jesus Christ in thought, word, deed and desire. When we become witnesses, we do not view witnessing as an activity confined to a special "invasion" or personal evangelism campaign. These activities are necessary and wonderful, but witness must characterize our lives.

TRUE WITNESSES, TRUE AFFECTIONS

Early Pentecostals were convinced that the power of God falls on the sanctified life just as the fire came down on Mount Carmel and consumed the sacrifice in response to Elijah's prayer (see 1 Kings 18:38). The fruit of the Spirit, or Christian affections, are essential to becoming and being a witness.

Affections are objective, relational and attitudinal. Take the chief Christian affection or fruit, *love*. For the Christian, love is no mere mood, feeling or passing fancy. Love is the very nature of God. It has objective existence.

Christian love is not manifested in the fact that we have loved God, but rather that He has loved us. He loved us in a particular way—He gave His Son for us. Love is a Christlike response to the world. Love which is truth corresponds to the love of God.

Christian love can exist only in a relationship with our God, who is love. What would it mean for us to say that we have Christian love without loving God? God is the continuing source of love. The great commandment to love God with all of our heart, soul and strength presupposes the second great commandment—loving our neighbors as ourselves.

Christian love always characterizes the true believer. In Matthew 25, people are caught being themselves when no one is looking. On Judgment Day, many will say, "Lord, when did we see You hungry . . . or naked . . . or in prison?" (v. 44). What they mean is, "Lord, if we had known it was You, we would have done something!"

The reward of heaven is not for those who do what they do because they seek a reward; it is for those who act in love. The Good Samaritan cared for the neighbor in the ditch. The true Christian cares for the hurting and needy in the world. In this way the true Christian is full of care, or one might say, careful to love as God loves. The true Christian must exercise stewardship of the love of God in his or her heart.

How can one's testimony be true if one's life is uneven? The watching world wants to know. If true Christian affections correspond with the reality of God, if they are kept alive only in vital relationship with God and neighbor, and if they truly come to characterize who we are, then Christian affections become the reasons we do what we do. Here are three examples.

CHRISTIAN GRATITUDE

Take the matter of Christian gratitude. To be ungrateful and to claim to be a Christian is a contradiction. The essence of salvation is grace. No one deserves to be saved; salvation comes only by grace through faith. It is the gift of God! This gratitude becomes the grace that we are to show to others. We are to forgive as we have been forgiven.

Gratitude, then, is a fundamental source of witness. We look on men and women in terms of sin and grace; we see them as God sees them. We seek to minister grace to our hearers. We look on those lost and in bondage, and say, "There, but for the grace of God, go I."

No one continually, absolutely and inexhaustibly does all of the will of God to the same degree that Jesus did the will of the Father on earth. Every Christian, then, needs the grace of God at every moment. If we know to do good and do not do it, it is sin to us (see James 4:17).

But this is no excuse for sin. What God looks for is a perfect reliance on His grace. This is why Paul can say, "Shall we . . . sin that grace may abound? Certainly not!" (Romans 6:1, 2). Our understanding is flawed and we have all kinds of fallibility and weaknesses, but God still graciously bears us along. To be thankless and unforgiving, therefore, contradicts all Christian testimony.

Sin is to be confronted and rebuked. But correction and instruction in righteousness must be given with long-suffering. Having said this, however, we must remember that it is God's will for no one to perish but that all should come to repentance (2 Peter 3:9).

CHRISTIAN COMPASSION

Consider the affection of compassion. This grace signifies that love has touched down somewhere in this world. Compassion is love that sees the world as God sees it. Jesus was moved with compassion when He looked upon the multitudes and saw them as sheep not having a shepherd (Matthew 9:36).

The love of God enables us to see the world differently than we did before. We no longer see men and women as trees walking, but as persons made in God's image. To be filled with the Spirit of love is to sigh and groan after God on behalf of those who do not know Him and who dwell in darkness.

Like gratitude, a God-like compassion is essential to a Christlike witness. The lack of love in our hearts becomes an occasion for the attack of the Enemy.

Love for the things of the world often fills hearts with so many cares that no time or room is left to receive others and care for them. We get caught up in the affairs of life and frustrated by its disappointments, both small and great. Our lives are busy, cluttered and driven.We soon find ourselves on the road with the priest and Levite and pass by the person in the ditch.

Those whose hearts are filled with compassion regularly name the names of others in prayer. Their praying ceases to be selfish. They become intercessors. A true intercessor moves among (the literal meaning of the word *intercessor*) those for whom he or she is interceding. Compassion is a motive, and a true motive moves one to act in a certain way.

To have compassion on the hungry and fail to feed them is a contradiction. To have compassion for the lost and fail to call them to repentance by the gospel is a contradiction in terms. Those who testify of a compassionate Savior must follow in His steps and walk as He walked, if their testimonies are to ring true.

CHRISTIAN COURAGE

Look at the quality of courage. If witnessing to the truth is a life-and-death matter in a world of lies and a culture of death, is it any wonder that we should be fearful before a watching world? Jesus promised that He would not leave us comfortless, but would send another Comforter.

This Comforter would be One like Himself who would abide with us, lead us, teach us and empower us to witness to the world in word and deed.

When we are filled with the Holy Spirit—the power that raised Jesus from the dead—we gain victory over the one who has the power of the fear of death. Satan and those who serve him threaten to kill all who bear witness to the truth. If he can, he will kill their influence and neutralize their activity on behalf of Jesus Christ, instead of killing them physically.

It is easy enough to bear witness to Christ in a culture which assumes that Christianity is a part of its heritage. But when a culture is like the culture of the Roman Empire's (many say that describes North America's culture today), being a witness to Christ becomes counter-cultural.

The world, the flesh and the devil oppose every powerful, compelling witness to the Christ who calls all to repentance. Only a bold faith can overcome the world (see 1 John 5:4). It takes a deep confidence and love for God to mortify the deeds of the flesh, for they compromise, dilute, detour and contradict a true witness of Christ.

For us to successfully resist the devil and the forces of hell, we have to have a quickening and an emboldening of the Holy Spirit. Gratitude and love alone are insufficient to overcome the opposition to witness in a hostile environment where one may be asked to give one's life at any moment for the testimony of Jesus Christ.

True Witnesses, True Lives

I have known people who exemplified such gratitude, compassion and courage in the face of seemingly overwhelming odds. They gave me gifts that I cannot begin to put a proper value on—gifts truly priceless.

Like Paul, I can look back and say that I am ready to die or live with such people (see Philippians 1:22-25). These people are living epistles . . . living in my heart (see 2 Corinthians 3:2, 3; 7:3). Their faces are treasured there.

Looking back, I can now understand how these people got into my heart and exercised such a tremendous influence in helping me become a witness today. As I mention a few, perhaps you will be reminded of several like them who have represented Christ to you and others in a powerful way.

Marie—A Witness in Worship and Serving

Marie was ugly by the world's standards, a poor woman labeled "mentally retarded," and loud in worship. She would wait until the choir finished singing and was marching from the platform to sit with the main congregation. At that precise moment, Marie would "go off" like an air-raid siren. She would raise her hands and clap them, and say "Glory, glory, glory" as tears streamed down her smiling face.

As I got to know Marie, I learned the meaning of those tears and that laughter. Though rarely visited by members of her family, Marie would reach out to others in the housing project where she lived. She would feed the hungry and share with those like herself who had little.

She prayed for and loved me and others in the church. We were her family. Gathering with the saints in worship was a foretaste of heaven to her. I believe that in heaven before God she was beautiful, rich and wise.

Marie gave me great gifts. Because of her, I learned to reject the cultural definition of beauty. Even today I despise the evaluation of others, whether based on outward appearance, wealth or intelligence. I know that these things were wrong because Marie was right.

My witness is what it is today because she taught me by faithfully living the principles of Christ. Marie was a powerful witness; she is in my heart forever.

LILLIAN JENKINS—A WITNESS IN SUFFERING

Lillian Jenkins must have had 5,000 hairpins in her hair! We kids concluded that she must be able to pick up faraway radio stations on those hairpins. Her hair looked like she had stuck her finger in a light socket and had been electrified, frizzing her hair all over.

Lillian would blink her eyes continuously during the service, and say under her breath the word *Jesus* over and over. Sometimes she would punctuate His name, JESUS!, startling the people around her and causing them to jump. She could be distracting, to say the least.

In a Wednesday night testimony service, I learned that her husband, an alcoholic, had hit her with his fist. She had a huge bruise on her face. With tears streaming down her face, she confessed what had happened and requested prayer for him.

The church council put feet on their prayers and visited her husband to inform him that they were praying for him. But they also told him that if he ever touched her again they would personally come, tie him up and take him to jail! This was real fellowship.

In later years he came to the Lord, due to the faithful, sanctifying witness of his wife and no doubt in some measure the tough love of the church. Lillian will always be in my heart as someone who exemplified long-suffering and faithfulness in the face of great adversity.

Brother John—A Witness in Caring

Brother John was a white-haired man who walked with two canes. His eyes were glazed with cataracts and his voice was hoarse and raspy. Usually he wore an old tattered coat, and hung his felt hat on a nail near the pew where he sat each Wednesday night.

In testimony he would recall the ordinary events of his week and comment on how good God was and how glad he was to be in a wonderful church family. He requested prayer for others. Often John walked to church down a busy highway. When the weather was adverse due to rain or extreme cold, Dad or someone else would go and pick him up.

I was drawn deeper into his life and finally his home, where I learned that John was caring for a wife who was diagnosed as schizophrenic. For more than 10 years he rose each morning, changed the bedclothes, gave her a bath, put clean clothes on her, fixed her breakfast, fed her, washed and rolled her hair, combed it out, and told her how beautiful she was! She would laugh and cry as he would kiss her and tell her how much he loved her.

Some weeks, John would be discouraged and cry. He would ask for added prayer to have the strength to care for his wife and live his witness in the community. But he never failed to say that he knew God would provide and be faithful to him.

I came to treasure every wrinkle and every crease in the weathered face of that old man.

All who knew Brother John knew he was a true Christian. His witness was noted throughout the church and in the community. When he died, people all over town said, "That man was a true Christian." You could not look at John and fail to think of Christ and His church.

Brother Theo—A Witness in Dying

If it ever seemed I was laughing or making fun of Brother Theo in any way, my father would give me that "look" that only he could give. The look meant that any disrespect to Theo would mean I would be taken to the basement of the church and "receive the right hand of fellowship across the seat of understanding!"

Theo had a cleft palate and people in town often laughed at him. They ridiculed and mocked him. He was shy and quick-tempered, but he was vulnerable and caring, too.

When Theo got cancer we all began to pray. We had seen many miraculous healings in the church. Indeed, my mom and dad—who are perhaps deeper in my heart than anyone in this world—often prayed for others who were healed.

Brother Theo would stand on Wednesday night and testify of God's goodness, even as he grew weaker day by day. Some weeks he was happy and testified that he believed the Lord had healed him. Other weeks he would be disappointed and sad. Then his sadness would change to anger, and he would voice that anger in the testimony service.

I remember going forward at the end of the service when I was a little boy, and joining others in laying hands on Brother Theo as we prayed for God to heal him.

One week Brother Theo stood with tears in his eyes and said that he was ready to meet the Lord. He said he believed the Lord was coming to take him.

In a few days, he said, he would be in the church again—not standing, but lying in a coffin. He praised the Lord and thanked Him for His goodness. He thanked everyone in the church for their faithfulness and their prayers.

Brother Theo died a few days later. Again, the church gathered at the front of the sanctuary. Standing around Brother Theo's coffin, we knew he was alive because we knew that Jesus was alive. The fellowship was not broken. Love was stronger than death!

Theo gave me a great gift in showing me how a Christian dies. God had given him courage. He gave his life to the Lord and shared it with us. I can't wait to see him again one day.

And Others

I could go on with a great list of those who have been witnesses to me and to many others. You can probably do the same—I hope you can! Witnesses to Christ carry with them faces of people whom they treasure in their hearts. True witnesses are also in the hearts of others.

The church is a company of witnesses, a missionary fellowship, which is characterized by these kinds of deep relationships. Nothing is uglier than an impersonal, highly individualistic witness. Even as there is no salvation outside the church (the body of Christ), so there is no authentic witness apart from the company of genuine witnesses in the world. None of us would be a Christian unless someone had born this witness to us.

These Christian witnesses still shine in my heart today. The light of Christ illumines their faces like an icon on a bright computer screen, or like the icon of a saint in an Eastern Orthodox church! They are the living epistles—the illustrated version of the Scriptures that I cherish.

God has their faces, and ours, in His heart. He cares for each of us. He longs for the whole world. The Spirit sighs and groans, along with the whole creation, awaiting the full and final manifestation of the sons and daughters of God coming into their own (see Romans 8:22, 23).

On that day when all worlds flash away and we, in a twinkling-eye moment, rise to meet Him, the faces of all the redeemed will shine with the glory of the Kingdom. As we approach the throne, I believe all the faces will coalesce as in a great, heavenly mosaic; and we shall see there in those faces the pattern of the face of God!

Let us look to Jesus and treasure new faces in our hearts by seeing our neighbors who are in need these, we do it to Him.

Christian witnesses are not parts of a faceless mob or a mindless mass. We are unique agents of His kingdom . . . called to bear witness in the court of the Judge of all the earth—who is also its Savior.

CHAPTER **5**

THE AWESOME POWER OF A TRUTHFUL LIFE

We have renounced the hidden things of shame, not walking in craftiness nor handling the word of God deceitfully, but by manifestation of the truth commending ourselves to every man's conscience in the sight of God

(2 Corinthians 4:2).

*T*here is practically no one, saint or sinner, who respects a hypocrite. What is a hypocrite? The literal meaning of *hypocrite* is "one who who speaks out from under a mask," or someone who is not what he or she seems.

In the language of everyday discourse we say that a hypocrite is one who doesn't "walk the talk." He or she claims one thing and does another. Clearly, such people can have a negative effect on others. This is why people often have such a low opinion of politicians, used-car salespersons—or even Christians for that matter!

When those who claim to be telling the truth about God, while calling on men and women around them to repent, live hypocritical, contradictory lives, then is it any wonder that the way of the truth is doubted or rejected? After hearing so many claims and being offered so many "sales pitches," many modern people ask, like Pilate of old, "What is truth?"

RATIONALE FOR A TRUTHFUL LIFE

Over the centuries, philosophers have developed various criteria for ascertaining the truth. Perhaps the three most well known are the *correspondence*, *coherence* and *viability* theories.

CORRESPONDENT TRUTH

In the discussion of a scientific hypothesis or a testimony in a courtroom, one will often hear various theories applied in determining the truth of statements about the nature of reality or about the case being deliberated in court.

Suppose someone says, "The sun is shining much brighter today than it did yesterday." To determine the truth of this statement, one would have to know how brightly the sun was shining yesterday, and compare it to today.

Further, one would have to look out the window to see if the sun was shining at all! In this way, one would determine whether the claim made corresponded to the reality of the sun shining on the days in question. The most obvious way to test claims to truth is to see whether it corresponds with the way the world actually is.

Of course, if one were blind or hidden away from the sun, it would be difficult for that person to determine the truth or falsity of the claim. Then, the individual would have to trust expert testimony or find other measures whereby one could compare the shining of the sun yesterday with today.

Coherent Truth

In addition to correspondent truth, there is *coherent* truth. Suppose someone testifies that they believe it is not going to rain today, but he or she puts on a raincoat before going outside—and takes an umbella along! This person's testimony doesn't hold together, or cohere, in a logical manner.

In the test of coherence, one is looking for inner contradictions that will discredit the claim to truth, or strong agreement among statements (coherence) that will support the claim to truth. Prosecutors usually have a field day finding internal contradictions in the testimony of witnesses. With strong coherence, there is a "ring of truth" to a statement.

VIABLE TRUTH

In addition to correspondence to reality and inner coherence, there is a third test of truth: *viability*. For something to be true, it has to withstand the test of viability, or the pragmatic test: Will it work? Often, scientific research or a theory seems logical, but when put to an actual test, it does not work.

This means that the research or theory does not take into account certain variables. A simple example will suffice. When the "on" button is pressed on a flashlight, a light pierces the darkness. But sometimes one picks up the flashlight in question, presses the button, and nothing happens.

The statement "When you push the 'on' button, the light will shine in the darkness," is viable only when there are batteries and a good bulb in the flashlight.

The situation becomes even more complicated when we are considering truth in relation to God and daily questions of right and wrong.

SCRIPTURAL TRUTH

To have a truthful life, we must know the only true God (John 17:3). When Moses sang a song of deliverance, he spoke of God as "a God of truth" (Deuteronomy 32:4). By this he meant that God judges in righteousness and there is no injustice in Him. He is utterly dependable and faithful.

Since God is ultimate reality, to know Him is to know the truth. Moses and those to whom God had revealed Himself over the years had found God to be dependable and faithful.

To the Hebrew mind, truth, faithfulness and dependability were interconnected. They were all a part of the same thing. To say that God was true meant to them that God was faithful and utterly reliable. Therefore, God's Word was also true and reliable. God's Word accomplished what God desired. His Word created reality and brought about redemption of reality when it was distorted by sin.

Problems arose when men and women were not true to God, or their words were untruthful. While things they spoke may have been factually accurate, if they used their knowledge to further a sinful cause, they were liars who did not practice the truth (see 1 John 1:6).

Jesus proclaimed in John 14:6, "I am the way, the truth, and the life." Therefore, to know the truth was to follow the way of Jesus Christ and to walk in His steps. The way of truth is synonymous with the way of life.

To walk in truth is to walk in light and life, and to walk in darkness is to walk in death. The truth of Jesus sets men and women free from the deception and delusions of sin. They are set free to love as God loves (John 8:32).

Paul speaks of the truth as being in Jesus (Ephesians 4:21), and claims that this "truth of Christ" is in himself (2 Corinthians 11:10). For Paul and all Christians after him, one could not know Christ truly without having truth in the inward parts.

Then, as now, the deceitfulness of the human heart and the desire to do one's own thing would prevent one from knowing the truth as the truth is in Jesus. Jesus told the scholars of His day that they searched the Scriptures because they thought they had eternal life in them, but the Scriptures testified of Him (John 5:39)!

Why wouldn't they come to Jesus? Because their deeds were evil. He said in 7:17 that anyone could know whether His teaching was from God or from man if that person truly wants to do the will of God. Someone trying to figure a way to do his or her own will, in spite of the will of God, will be the victim of endless doubts and questions.

Just as Jesus bore witness to the truth in His person and word, so the Holy Spirit is the Spirit of truth who convinces the world of sin, righteousness and judgment (16:8). The Spirit leads those who are willing to follow into all truth.

Scripture claims to offer a witness that corresponds to the reality of God, God's creation and redemption. The Scriptures are coherent and have a central meaning in Jesus Christ. They all testify to Him. Scripture is a light in the path of those who want to follow in the way of Jesus by the leading and power of the Holy Spirit.

It is the Spirit who inspired and inspires the Scriptures. Scripture, in turn, witnesses to Jesus Christ.

He then forms men and women, whose character and deeds glorify the Father in heaven. So what does it mean to lead a truthful life?

THE REALITY OF A TRUTHFUL LIFE

KNOWING THE TRUTH

According to the Bible, one can know accurate facts but still be a false person. The devil and the demons knew that Jesus was the Son of God, but they were not living in the truth. The devil is a liar. He takes accurate facts and twists them into lies and deception.

In the temptation of Jesus in the wilderness (Matthew 4), he repeatedly said to Jesus, "If You are the Son of God. . . ." In this way the devil takes what he knows to be true and twists it so that he can tempt God rather than worship Jesus.

When one knows Biblical truth, the person is free. But this freedom is not the freedom to do as one pleases. It is the freedom to obey God in love.

When my oldest daughter was in elementary school, her teacher asked the class to tell their parents' names and give their occupations. My daughter said, "My mother is Peggy and she is a teacher. My daddy is Steve and he studies God."

Later that afternoon I received a call from her teacher. She wanted to know how one went about studying God. My reply to her was, "Very carefully."

We cannot study God without being studied by

God. To know God is to be changed, confronted, judged, and offered grace. We cannot study God the way we study a star, a rock or a chemical compound; the study of God is self-involving. To know the truth of God is to have one's life tested for truth. It is to come to a dead halt: "Be still, and know that I am God" (Psalm 46:10).

During the 1960s, the matter of racial integration in public schools was a huge controversy in the South. The issue was more than the placing of black and white children in the same rooms; it had to do with the truth about the nature of a truly democratic society. It had to do with the truth about the equality of human beings.

The United States Declaration of Independence speaks of all men being "created equal." The Founders debated and struggled over the question of slavery at the beginning of this country, and the nation fell into, and practiced, heinous slavery. Both the North and the South benefited economically from the abomination of the merchandising of humankind.

The true issue was this: To integrate the races would not mean the assimilation or obliteration of distinctions. Rather, it would mean all the people dwelling together in diversity, learning together, respecting one another and envisioning a common future as a nation.

If one determines to love certain neighbors and not others, or to love neighbors differently based on the color of their skin, then one has a segregated heart and integration can never be true for that person. One has to know the truth in the inward parts.

The truth sets us free to truly love. To know God as Creator is to know that fellow humans are made in God's image and are therefore persons to be loved as God loves them. To know and believe this truth sets one free from the ugliness of segregation and slavery.

Loving the Truth

One must not only know the truth but must love it. We cannot continue to see and know the truth clearly without loving it. This is because we cannot know God without loving God.

The knowledge of God is an intimate thing. Adam knew Eve, who conceived and bore sons. We must speak of this kind of intimate, fruitful knowing when we speak of knowing God.

To know God means that Christ has been formed in us and we are born again from above. The Holy Spirit sheds the love of God abroad in our hearts so that we might rejoice in the truth and not in iniquity.

According to John, God is truth and God is love (1 John 4:6-8). Therefore we cannot become a truthful person without being a loving person. Those who know the true God will begin to correspond to God not only in the words they say but also in their hearts. They will evidence the fruit of the Spirit of truth (Galatians 5:22, 23). This fruit will begin to characterize their lives.

Only one of the two participants in the drama of Jesus' temptation in the desert loved the truth because only one of them had come to do the will of the Father (see Matthew 4; Luke 4). The truth of God must rule over, correct, expose, and drive out all other claims of truth.

People who know and love God love His Word. They love His Word even when it cuts and hurts. A false witness claims to know God while embracing a lie.

WALKING IN TRUTH

If we truly know and love our spouse, we will behave in a loving way toward our spouse. If we truly know and love our brother and sister in Christ, we will speak the truth in love and not grieve the Holy Spirit through evil speaking (see Ephesians 4:15-32).

One must not only know and love the truth but also walk in the truth. It is easy to deceive ourselves. If we truly know and love the truth, we will walk in it.

To become a truthful person then is to know the true God and to walk in the truth because one has a true heart. Having the truth of God in our inward parts means that our minds think upon the truth, our hearts love the truth, and our wills surrender to the truth.

PRACTICING TRUTH

Some say they love, but their lives are, in fact, a lie (see Revelation 22:15). The Bible tells us they will not enter into the gates of the Holy City and enjoy the fellowship of the New Jerusalem. There is much talk of love today, but unless it is a love born of the knowledge of the True and Holy One, it will not be acceptable to God.

Some, like the Good Samaritan, may not know much about God, but they act on what they know. These will be accepted by God and will go into the Kingdom ahead of those who pay lip service to the Scripture but do not practice its truth.

The worst people mentioned in Matthew 25 will go away into everlasting torment, and will do so because they were caught being themselves. They knew what the Scriptures said about the hungry, the naked, the stranger and the prisoners; but they did not practice the truth toward them. They did not love them as God loves them.

One may even quote Scripture and tell a lie because he or she does not quote the Word in love. The devil did this. The truth spoken in love builds up the body of Christ. This truth in each heart and life and embodied in the local church always brings unfailing results.

The Results of a Truthful Life

Forgiveness

To be forgiven and to forgive is at the heart of the truthful life. All have sinned. None comes to repentance without the mercy and drawing of God. The Christian life, from start to finish, is predicated on the grace of God; so to be unforgiving is to live a lie. Confession and true repentance are necessary before forgiveness can be received and enjoyed.

Deeply spiritual individuals understand, especially when seeking to restore another who has fallen into sin, that they too are frail and temptable. They know and recognize that they are what they are only by the grace of God.

Pride goes before a fall because it is based on the lie of self-sufficiency. Those who are merciful, who forgive as God forgives, will obtain mercy because God is merciful. Their practice of mercy corresponds to the mercy of God and is consistent with its operation in their own lives. It is the consistent practice of a grateful heart.

SANCTIFICATION

God sanctifies us through the truth. Knowing, loving and walking in truth continually sanctifies the believer (see John 17:17, 19). Jesus, who was truth Himself, bore witness to the truth of God and offered Himself on Calvary. He sanctified Himself! He did this so that we could be sanctified in the truth. This is the only truth that makes us free!

The truth of redemption in Jesus Christ sanctifies the believer so that he or she offers up a sacrifice by the Holy Spirit through the Lord Jesus Christ himself. In this way, the believer testifies that he or she is crucified with Christ.

This means that one's deeds, words, desires, hopes, fears, values, behavior—one's whole being—is offered to God as a living sacrifice (Romans 12:1, 2). A passionate devotion to God should characterize the normal Christian life. This would mean the end of "nominal" Christianity.

To believe that Jesus was crucified for the sins of the world is to be crucified with Him. To believe that

He was raised to newness of life means that one is also raised and lives by the power of that new life in the Spirit. This is clearly more than a mere assent to certain propositions. It requires the continual power of the Spirit of truth.

Being hateful or stirring up hate in others, being lustful or stirring up lust in others, being dishonest and encouraging dishonesty in others—these are contradictions of a truthful Christian life. They are all indicative of deeds of the flesh, which must be killed (crucified or mortified) and replaced with the fruit of the Spirit. Thus, sanctification is whole-hearted devotion to God.

When one is sanctified, one loves what God loves and hates what God hates. One rejoices in the truth and not in iniquity. Truth and righteousness are correlated in the same way iniquity and a lie are correlated.

One who lives in humble gratitude and whole-hearted love to God and neighbor will continually invoke the power of the Holy Spirit to give a witness that is powerful and effective before a watching world.

A LIFE OF POWER

Since this truth corresponds to the will of God for the salvation of all people, a truthful witness longs for the salvation of those whom he or she encounters. A gracious, compassionate witness is a compelling one. The Holy Spirit speaks through such a life to convince the world of sin, righteousness and judgment.

Truth is more than mere propositions or factual statements; it is the redemptive reality in Christ which He makes possible in the believer. For this reason, those who are witnesses to the truth will shine as lights in the darkness. Their lives will be so powerful that their words, influence and deeds will be used to bring others to the redemptive reality we call salvation.

The righteousness, peace and joy of the kingdom of God begins to characterize the lives of those who live a truthful life. This enables them, by the Holy Spirit, to change their own surrounding reality.

A truthful life does nothing against the truth, only for it. Others may reject, deny or work against the truth of God in Christ, but the true witness knows that this opposition is doomed to failure. The assurance and confidence of the truthful witness makes his or her testimony powerful before the menacing world and the devil.

The world is overcome through the faith and faithfulness of the true witness. The devil is overcome with a humble resistance from the true witness (see Revelation 12:11). Because of continual sanctification and wholehearted devotion to God, a true witness is a clear channel for the Spirit's empowerment.

Often the greatest hindrance to the church and the world is the church itself. Why are so many congregations weak? Why do they fail to be redemptive and prophetic in society? Why are they afraid to take on any trouble? Can it be because they are failing to walk in unity in the light of the Scriptures?

Here is the key to true fellowship. It is not in perfectly understanding every scripture or perfectly applying God's truth every moment of every day. It is to be seeking to walk in the light of Scripture that we continue to understand as the Lord gives us light and understanding.

It is not the difficult scriptures that hinder the church in the world today; it is, instead, those scriptures the church understands too well . . . verses like these:

- "Love one another; as I have loved you" (John 13:34).
- "Bear one another's burdens" (Galatians 6:2).
- "Comfort one another" (1 Thessalonians 4:18).
- "Restore one another" (see Galatians 6:1).
- "Confess your [sins] to one another" (James 5:16)."
- "Convince, rebuke, exhort, with all long-suffering and teaching" (2 Timothy 4:2).

The Bible promises us that "if we walk in the light as He is in the light, we [will] have fellowship with one another," and his blood will keep on cleansing us from all unrighteousness (1 John 1:7). The light of God is powerful, but we must walk in it if we are to shine brightly and love deeply out of pure hearts.

When Christians speak the truth together in love, they grow up into Christ in all things and have a powerful and mature witness before a watching world (see Ephesians 4:15). When Christians live together truthfully, the way of truth ceases to be spoken of in an evil way.

Men and women in society today are dying for true community. The church should be provoking them to jealousy as the watching world sees how believers love one another in true fellowship. A consistent, gracious, compassionate Spirit-filled life has awesome power because it is God who witnesses through such a life.

THE RENDERING OF A TRUTHFUL LIFE

Each believer must render to God that loving obedience which leads to a truthful, consistent witness. We have all known people who lived such powerful lives. We know those whose very lives have been a condemnation of evil and whose very conversation seemed to change whatever setting they found themselves.

Jack Land had heard and seen the light of the gospel early in his life, but he did not become a Christian until after he married. He was a strong, rugged, deliberate man who trained hand-to-hand combat soldiers in World War II.

As Jack looked on his first child in the hospital nursery, God spoke to him for the first time in his life. He heard the Lord tell him he would be held accountable for how he raised this child. He waited some time before he told his wife about this, and he told no one else.

Jack was a deeply sober and loyal man. His mother-in-law, a Methodist, received the Holy Spirit baptism before there was a Pentecostal church in her town, and later became a charter member of the Church of God there. Before she died, she made him promise he would take his wife and son to visit the Church of God.

Jack attended the Church of God during a revival, and in a footwashing service God touched his heart. Although other Christians in his family discouraged it, he continued to attend the Church of God. He and his wife became members and were sanctified and filled with the Holy Spirit.

As his two children grew, they experienced the stability and regularity of a home where Christ was honored daily.

One Sunday night Jack stayed home from church because he wasn't feeling well. He began to throw up blood due to a massive, ulcerative hemorrhage that threatened his life. The son, whom he had been taking to church and who had recently been converted, heard his father's sigh in the bathroom and rose to go to him.

That night the boy laid his hands on Jack's head and prayed for his father: "Jesus, please heal my dad." God healed him, and bonded the father and son together in a deep way. Jack's son and a daughter grew up in a home where the gifts of the Spirit were honored and regularly manifested.

Jack and his wife were regular in attendance at the house of God, in family prayers, in tithing and giving, and in witnessing and serving in the community. They both worked six days a week. Jack would often work when he was sick, and go to church the same way, trusting the Lord for all things.

He was known in the community as a truthful man

who paid his debts, raised his children well, loved his family and tried to help others. The truth of the gospel affected all of his relationships. When workers were being treated unfairly and were being required to work too many hours with little or no home life, he helped to organize a union.

When it was clear that the schools were to be integrated, Jack joined a black principal and local pastors, both black and white, to pray that there would not be anyone hurt in what was then the most violent county in his Southern state.

Jack and his wife were well known and respected throughout the Christian and Jewish communities. They were known as men and women of prayer and goodwill whose word and life could be trusted.

Jack's son and daughter grew up with a sense of pride in the good name and reputation of their parents. When his wife briefly withdrew from the church because of its legalism and harshness, Jack maintained his faithfulness to her and to the church. He knew that God had led them there, and He was not finished with His purpose for them through that ministry.

God spoke to him one day, and Jack sold everything and moved his family to a much larger city. They moved to a social environment much different from what they were accustomed. Within weeks, Jack was witnessing and praying with criminals, transvestites, homosexuals, drug addicts, and hundreds of young people searching to find meaning in their lives. Again, he worked night and day and was a rock of faithfulness as a bi-vocational minister in an inner-city mission.

Some years later, after 15,000 people had been blessed in the residential program of his mission, a church was organized. Out of it, three others were planted. Many interns were trained in ministry, and scores of men and women were discipled and sent to other churches.

One day Jack fell on a slippery floor in a department store. He suffered a severe internal head injury which greatly hastened his aging and made him dependent on his devoted wife. Today, Jack lies suspended between this world and the next, but he still wants to minister. In moments of clarity, he prays for his children and grandchildren. Even in his weakness, he is still a powerful witness to all with whom he comes in contact.

Although Jack doesn't understand why this has happened to him at this place in his life, in his depression, there is joy. In his pain, there is praise. In patiently waiting, there is a constant giving of suffering love to those about him.

Often, in the early hours of the morning he struggles with basic bodily functions. As his wife ministers to him, she will look into his eyes and see the gaze of the One who is *the* truthful witness . . . Jesus Christ.

This truthful witness is my father, loyal and faithful still. He is a rock of dependability. Though reduced virtually to skin and bones, he is more powerful now than ever. His life has taken on the shape of the life of the Savior Himself, as he makes himself available to be used of God each day.

In the Spirit, Jack Land continually prays for others and awaits the coming of his Lord who has promised He would receive him soon.

My father has not understood every scripture in the Bible perfectly, but he has practiced every one he knew to the utmost ability God has given him. He has been a good and faithful servant, and my best friend.

He is also my most perfect example that I can find of living a truthful life on earth.

Nothing can overcome the awesome power of a truthful life that testifies to Jesus Christ. May each of our lives and the story we relate to our generation tell the truth and tell it well!

CHAPTER 6

LIVING AND DYING
BY YOUR
TESTIMONY

You are no longer strangers and for-eigners, but fellow citizens with the saints and members of the household of God, . . . built on the foundation of the apostles and prophets, Jesus Christ Himself being the chief cornerstone, in whom the whole building . . . grows into a holy temple in the Lord . . . for a dwelling place of God in the Spirit (Ephesians 2:19-22).

*S*everal years ago I was invited to speak in a Christian youth rally on the campus of Louisiana State University. A number of students responded and were praying at the altar when I noticed a small group to the left of the platform trying to get my attention. I responded.

A young lady, the spokesperson for the group, said, "When you began your message, we thought we were going to like you."

Obviously, that is not what a speaker wants to hear from someone in the audience.

"What happened?" I asked.

"Well," she began, "when you started your message, you talked about current events. You even threw in the words of a few contemporary songs to which we could easily relate. But you ended up like all the other preachers—talking about 'pie in the sky in the sweet bye and bye.' Don't tell us about the hereafter; we want to know about the here and now."

I went to my room with those words burning in my mind. Frankly, I was a little discouraged. In prayer that night, however, the Holy Spirit whispered a more pertinent message to my heart—one from which I have never recovered. He said, "Unless you want to stagger through the gloom of a senseless existence, you had better keep your focus on eternity."

The Book of Hebrews gives valuable insight into the hereafter: "Therefore He [Christ] is also able to save to the uttermost those who come to God through Him,

since He always lives to make intercession for them"
(7:25). These are precious words, but I want you to
focus on two phrases—"save to the uttermost" and
"He always lives."

ASKING THE QUESTIONS

It is wonderful to have help and hope now, and
maybe even for the foreseeable future. Sooner or
later, however, we come face-to-face with *what then.*
What happens after we are saved?

Our testimonies as Christian believers are always
relevant because they get to the big questions: *Who
but our Lord offers hope forever? Who besides our triumphant, risen Lord lives forever to carry out His promises?*

From any true perspective the Christian story is
one of eternal dimensions. It is the story of God's
plan for humankind in terms of the big picture. Of
necessity the story deals with the ups and downs of
life, its pains and pleasures, its prosperity and pov-
erty.

But if it didn't offer something beyond that, if it
didn't speak to the big question of eternity, then it
would not be worthy of our time and effort.

The story we live by, the cause for which we
give ourselves on a daily basis—year in and year
out—has to be one we're also willing to die by. If
not, we are deceived and we are deceiving others.
Only God truly knows what is in the heart, and He
will be the ultimate judge. It is critically important
for each of us as true believers to live out the story

of God and to hold ourselves accountable to others.

QUESTIONS OF FAITH

The young people mentioned in the opening paragraph of this chapter, and so many like them, are ensnared in a culture of the present, the immediate, the reality of life now. They remind us that few come to peace and faith without a struggle.

Unfortunately, it may be that we as a church have been too slow to acknowledge the doubts, the midnight questionings of our soul, the lonely sojourns into despair. In a sense, we may have tried so hard to convince our children of the truths of the story and the rewards of the journey that we neglected to share the hard lessons of faith.

An honest faith is most often a questioning one. There is no reason to fear a questioning faith. The Bible is full of stories about those who voiced their doubts and questioned not only their faith but also the very decrees and purposes of God.

Gideon is an excellent example. Like a lot of young people today, he was raised on all the wonderful stories of what God had done, but he wondered where was that same God now. Remember Gideon's interchange with the angel?

> The Angel of the Lord appeared to him, and said to him, "The Lord is with you, you mighty man of valor!"
>
> Gideon said to Him, "O my lord, if the Lord is

with us, why then has all this happened to us? And where are all His miracles which our fathers told us about, saying, 'Did not the Lord bring us up from Egypt?'" (Judges 6:12, 13).

Gideon struggled with his faith, but thank God, he managed to rise above the doubts. He listened to God, took the first small step and then went on to triumphant victory. This is the way doubts are transformed into stepping stones of faith.

Questions of Logic

When was the last time you faced up to some of the troubling questions? Have you ever asked: What profit is there in serving God? Is there an absolute for human beings? Why should I be moral when those who don't seem to care about morality appear to be getting along as well as—and some even better than—those who do?

These questions are often asked by human logic. The Word of God transcends human logic, however, with questions far more important. Questions such as the following:

- Do I know what it is to live in the presence of God?

- Do I have an unyielding confidence in God that He is with me and that He will never leave me?

- Do I understand the relational demands of Christianity?

- Do I have the calm assurance that even if

my circumstances do not prevail, my faith in God will?

One of the greatest needs of our time is for us to get a clear picture of the real meaning of the Christian life. There is no guesswork in Christianity. God wants us to follow Him with eyes open wide to the expectations and the challenges before us.

Books attempt to answer tough questions about God and His dealings with humankind. Some of them leave us with deep, sinking feelings as they postulate that all God has done is to get Creation off to a reasonably good start and then disappear. In most such books there is no recognition of a personal God.

But we know better. We know that God has revealed Himself in our lives in ways that are nothing short of supernatural.

QUESTIONS ABOUT SUFFERING

What we do not understand, and certainly cannot explain, is why He has chosen to reveal Himself in some situations and not in others. Edwin Young speaks to this aspect of faith:

> When calamity comes, we cry, "Oh, God, why has all this happened to me? I am losing my faith." Such a statement reveals that our faith has not truly been in God. Instead, it has been in what God could do for us! When we suffer the loss of God's _help_, we say we are losing our faith. In reality, our faith has been in our well-being. If our

faith were truly in God, we could lose everything else and still have faith. When our faith is in our own well-being, we cry, "Oh, God, don't You care? I am losing my faith in You." [8]

What a convicting thought. Is it possible that the faith we have defined for ourselves is faith in our own well-being rather than faith in a sovereign God? How much trouble and sickness would cause us to abandon faith altogether? How much more difficulty would it take for us to look elsewhere for solutions? Harold Kushner warns:

> The misfortunes of good people are not only a problem to the people who suffer and to their families. They are a problem to everyone who wants to believe in a just and fair and livable world. They inevitably raise questions about the goodness, the kindness, even the existence of God. [9]

Unfortunately, too many Christians have adopted a definition of faith that is far too narrow. Faith is not something you pick up when you need it and lay down when you don't. Faith is something you choose, and is to be with you continually.

An agnostic businessman was asked, "How did you lose your faith?"

"Lose my faith?" he responded. "I didn't lose it. I just put it away in a drawer and decided I would pull it out when I needed it. But when I went back for it, it wasn't there."

FINDING THE ANSWERS

Faith keeps you going, whether in the darkness

or in the sunshine. Faith keeps you believing in the grace, mercy and sovereignty of God—even in the midst of depressing circumstances. It is not a leap in the dark; but if you wait until you get everything figured out, you will never move.

Faith divorced from knowledge is mere superstition, yet faith is more than a mere assent to the facts. In Biblical terms, faith is belief. It is being convinced that certain things are true. Faith is trusting in God that He is always in charge and that He will always prevail, regardless of circumstances.

Faith is acting on what you believe. What is truth? Whom can I believe? How can I be sure I'm right? What if I'm wrong—not just in insignificant matters, but where it really counts? Can I ever settle all of my questions and doubts? Is this a lifetime challenge? Questions never end.

Yet, we are taught—or at least it is implied—that such questions should never be entertained. Faith that is never challenged, tested or questioned is a fragile faith. It is an immature faith and one that has little chance of surviving critical times.

FACE REALITY

Find the person who has never questioned his or her faith and you'll find someone whose faith is an illusion. On the other hand, find the individual who has been wrestled to the floor by doubt and who has climbed to his or her feet again, still believing and trusting God, and you will have a person who knows the real meaning of faith.

In these times it is essential for us to be confident regarding the certainties of the Christian faith. It is time for Christians to stop wasting so much energy on nonessentials, time to stop wandering in the wilderness of dried-up experiences. Too often we are too fast, too sore and too slow to anchor. We must find firm ground on which to stand, and follow Paul's advice:

> Stand therefore, having girded your waist with truth, having put on the breastplate of righteousness, and having shod your feet with the preparation of the gospel of peace; above all, taking the shield of faith with which you will be able to quench all the fiery darts of the wicked one. And take the helmet of salvation, and the sword of the Spirit, which is the word of God; praying always with all prayer and supplication in the Spirit, being watchful to this end with all perseverance and supplication for all the saints (Ephesians 6:14-18).

Be Genuine

We cannot afford to try to fake it. Too much is at stake. God's story cannot really be faked, and our testimonies are too important to be taken lightly. Our frantic faith must be replaced by a calm assurance that the Evil One will not prevail. These circumstances are under God's control. Our uncertainties are human and are but for the moment. God's promises are sure and certain.

The Christian life at its best is designed for us to live in an ongoing relationship with Jesus Christ.

We must live our testimonies out truthfully, in such a way that our hearts are more receptive to love God and our neighbors each day.

We know and understand from the Lord's inter-action with the thief on the cross that deathbed repentance is possible. It is probably more rare than we'd like to think, however. If someone plots for years on how _to use_ God and _cheat_ the devil at the last minute, then it seems far more likely the per-son will not wish to repent and serve God in the final few hours or days of life.

The human heart tends to become hardened through the deceitfulness of sin (Hebrews 3:13). How we live is usually an accurate indication of how we will die. If we have been walking in the light—in the direction of the Kingdom—then that light will grow brighter and the Kingdom will be-come more real with every passing day.

LIVE TRIUMPHANTLY

Unfortunately, many proclaim a _pick-and-choose_ gospel, emphasizing only parts of the Bible. They love and place great emphasis on promises, positives, vic-tories and beautiful stories. But they never seem to have read of punishment, retribution, sin, justice and judgment on evil. God's Word clearly and with-out apology sets forth both aspects, and it is impor-tant for God's children to live out the whole Bible.

God desires to bless His children. Scripture clearly reminds us that His compassion care and best wishes for us exceed any love impulse we as humans have for our own children. Jesus asked this question:

> "If you sinful people know how to give good gifts
> to your children, how much more will your
> heavenly Father give good gifts to those who
> ask him" (Matthew 7:11, *NLT*).

The Word of God lets us know, however, that God
will punish and discipline when necessary. He nudges
His children *onto* and *along* the straight and narrow
way.

LEARNING THE LESSONS

The writer of Hebrews addresses this aspect of
God's character in three explicit passages. He opens
the book by noting that God spoke in times past
through the prophets, through the angels, and with
many miracles. Now God has spoken most clearly
through the life and ministry of His own dear Son,
Jesus Christ.

> Therefore we must give the more earnest
> heed to the things we have heard, lest we drift
> away. For if the word spoken through angels
> proved steadfast, and every transgression and
> disobedience received a just reward, how shall
> we escape if we neglect so great a salvation,
> which at the first began to be spoken by the
> Lord, and was confirmed to us by those who
> heard Him (Hebrews 2:1-3).

In the third chapter, the writer makes a graphic com-
parison between what happened to the children of Israel
and what can most certainly happen to believers *when*
and *if* we take lightly the responsibility of living out the
testimony:

Therefore, as the Holy Spirit says: "Today, if you will hear His voice, do not harden your hearts as in the rebellion, in the day of trial in the wilderness, where your fathers tested Me, tried Me, and saw My works forty years. Therefore I was angry with that generation, and said, 'They always go astray in their heart, and they have not known My ways.' So I swore in My wrath, 'They shall not enter My rest'" (3:7-11).

The warning is so graphically clear that one wonders how so many hirelings of the gospel have nerve enough to ignore it. Note these words:

Beware, brethren, lest there be in any of you an evil heart of unbelief in departing from the living God; but exhort one another daily, while it is called "Today," lest any of you be hardened through the deceitfulness of sin. For we have become partakers of Christ if we hold the beginning of our confidence steadfast to the end (vv. 12-14).

As God's children in a skeptical and idolatrous age, we are called and commissioned not only to receive His blessings, but also to become instruments of His grace and blessings to the world. To help us accomplish this, God wills that we become ever more like the Master.

ENDURE THE SUFFERING

Often, this entails lessons in the school of suffering and the pain of carrying a cross. The Bible is replete with stories of good people who suffered. Brennan Manning notes in his book *Ruthless Trust*: "The Book of Job and the Psalms of lament show no interest in exculpating God from responsibility for the tragedy and misery of human existence."[10]

We may not wish to dwell on Job sitting in sackcloth and ashes . . . or on Paul being beaten and scourged, and constantly in prison . . . or on John the Baptist beheaded at the request of an adulterous mother and her dancing daughter . . . or on Deacon Stephen's final words while being stoned by an angry mob. But those too are testimonies of the saints. These, too, make up *God's story.*

Each of us have yet to comprehend the precise nature of our own sojourn. What we *can know,* and what we *do know* is that God has called us to live out the message of His love and to proclaim its validity in a grand finale of faith in the face of death itself.

BEAR THE CROSS

When our lives on earth are finally over, for what will we be remembered? That we drove the latest automobile? That we lived in a very nice home? That we made lots and lots of money? That we held high office in the city, county, state or nation? I find none of these things listed in our Lord's end-time commendations.

Instead, I read where He speaks of saints who have lived out *the story,* and whose testimony is associated with feeding the hungry, giving a drink to the thirsty, taking in the stranger, putting clothes on the naked, visiting the sick and befriending those cast into prison (Matthew 25:35, 36).

In this nation of freedoms, good times and blessedness, it seems so easy for God's children to be lulled into a semiconscious state of gracelessness, one that makes us forget the *life and death* decision that becoming a Christian entails. God's demands are no less simply because there is no dictator or government power breathing down our necks.

The invitation to follow Christ still comes in somber tones. It is still a lifelong, eternal proposition—*the story* of the ages:

> "If anyone desires to come after Me, let him deny himself, and take up his cross, and follow Me. For whoever desires to save his life will lose it, but whoever loses his life for My sake will find it. For what profit is it to a man if he gains the whole world, and loses his own soul? Or what will a man give in exchange for his soul?" (Matthew 16:24-26).

NURTURE THE COMMITMENT

The Christian life is not a light and easy proposition for young or old. It is not a commitment to be taken casually. Then again, where else are there promises that relate *to the uttermost?* Or challenges that equip us to live forever in the presence of the King of Glory?

Through the years, millions have found Christ to be a glorious and wonderful Lord to follow. He more than makes up for any perceived hardships. He more than compensates for any pain or difficulty.

Think of Stephen looking up while being stoned, and saying, "I see Jesus, standing at the right hand of God" (see Acts 7:55). When Paul was ready to die by a Roman executioner's sword, he wrote these words:

I have fought the good fight, I have finished the race, I have kept the faith. Finally, there is laid up for me the crown of righteousness, which the Lord, the righteous Judge, will give to me on that Day, and not to me only but also to all who have loved His appearing (2 Timothy 4:7, 8).

To live out the story of Christianity will cost us. It could cost us life itself. In fact, this is happening far more than most of us realize—even today. Research indicates there have been more Christian martyrs in the 20th century and up until now in the 21st than in all previous 1,900 years since Christ was born.

LIVING THE STORY

Iris Browning Vest grew up in a Christian home. She knew Christ all of her life. She married her childhood sweetheart, the only sweetheart she ever loved. She reared her children in the nurture and admonition of the Lord and continued to love them and her grandchildren each day. Her husband trusted and confided in her for everything.

Iris bore the grace and wisdom of a woman whose beauty and wisdom came from the Lord. She touched all with whom she came in contact. She was strong and fierce in her devotion to family and to the cause of Christ.

She was no pushover. Instead, her meekness expressed itself in bold witness as well as in gentle encouragement.

Why would one like this have a circulatory defect leading to multiple stints being placed in the vessels around her heart? Why would she have to live her last years never knowing when a vessel might be blocked and her life cut off? Why would she develop pancreatic cancer and have it successfully removed surgically—only to be killed by massive infection due to an unanticipated complication?

Iris faced these things as she lived her life—she faced death with faith. She placed herself squarely in the hands of God. She did not want to die; she did not want to leave her life's partner and her devoted children. But she went home.

God took her; it was not the devil. She lived her life weeping and rejoicing and placing trust in God for others; this is what she did in the face of death.

On September 11, 2001, thousands of men and women went to work in the twin towers of New York's World Trade Center and the Pentagon. Before the day was over, thousands died.

They, too, died as they had lived. If they had hardened their hearts toward God, perhaps they fled fearfully down the stairs with a hardened heart. Those men and women with stirrings of grace or a tendency to pray probably cried out to the Lord.

Some exited the building safely, others were crushed. Where was God in all of this? He saw the planes, He saw the people. God could have stopped these attempts. Other attempts had been thwarted—but not this time!

God sent a wake-up call to America in general

and to the church in particular: Wake up and pray together! Wake up and bear witness to the truth! Wake up and realize that every good blessing comes from God! Wake up and realize that the way you live is the way you will die. Wake up and repent of evil, and turn to righteousness. For "righteousness exalts a nation" (Proverbs 14:34), but the nation that forgets God will be turned into hell (Psalm 9:17).

Terrorists who lived in deception died in deception. The people who lived in faith died in faith. The people who lived in unbelief and hardness of heart died in unbelief and hardness of heart. God speaks to the nations, reminding them not to fear the one who can destroy the body but to fear the One who can destroy the body and soul in hell (Matthew 10:28).

The world presses for international peace, prosperity and order, contending it must do away with all religious distinctions and develop a universal religion of humankind. Christians who claim there is salvation in only one name given among men under heaven are on a collision course with such a world order.

Jesus said, "My kingdom is not of this world. If My kingdom were of this world, My servants would fight" (John 18:36). Sometimes we must fight to defend the weak. Sometimes we must fight to keep the innocent from being slaughtered. But our fighting will not bring the kingdom of God.

Only a truthful testimony of Jesus Christ, empowered by the Holy Spirit, will bring about the new birth which promises a kingdom of righteousness, joy and eternal peace. The Kingdom is already at work in the world, and will be fully realized everywhere, when one day everything is holiness unto the Lord.

Until that day, like Iris Vest, my late wife, and all the other faithful believers who die from disease, violence or acts of nature, let us not seek to gain our life, but to lose it for Christ's sake. Now is the time for sacrificial witness and service.

Now is the time to reclaim our testimonies in words and deeds of powerful witness.

Where is God in all of this? He is in the midst of all things. He is working them together for the good of those who love Him and are called according to His purpose. The death of His saints is precious in His sight, and their life of testimony lives after them in the lives and testimonies of those whom they have touched.

What do any of us have that we didn't receive? If we received it as a gift from God, how can we boast?

We who have received so much from so many must now pass it on!

Epilogue

Telling God's story fills you with gratefulness and gives meaning to life. Tell His story often enough and with enough passion, and you too will have a testimony to give and a story to tell.

*N*ow is the time to recover our testimony. It is time for each of us to review the stories of our journey and honor those faces in our hearts—the faces that represent the care, mercy and strength of the Lord for us.

Who are those special people whose prayers and influence have brought you to where you are today . . . and without whom you would not be in the Way?

Get the story straight. Find your place in it. More than ever we need to be steeped in all the truth of Scripture. There are so many diverse stories in the world that unless Christians know and communicate daily in relevant ways the story of the Holy Bible, its message will be lost or ignored. We are no longer live in a Biblical culture, rather we are in a culture of astounding Biblical ignorance.

In such a milieu we must live the truthful life which integrates head, heart and hand, or our knowing, our being and our doing. Knowledge we gain about God leads to the strengthening of our characters and to Christian deeds consistent with that knowledge and character.

We must begin to form small groups in the church that carry out mission tasks together as a team, holding each other accountable and reliable as we seek to inspire one another to love and good works.

We must realize that we are on a journey together. We must cease trying to parade before the watching world. We must reject the modern Baal gods of beauty, brains, brawn and bucks. We must not spend time at beauty contests or in judging who is the smartest, strongest or richest among us.

Rather than compete with one another, we must re-learn what it means to be laborers together. Our witness must become a life-and-death matter once again.

The 20th century was the bloodiest century in all of Christian history. Thousands of Christians are already suffering martyrdom, imprisonment and persecution around the world. I believe that these same trials are coming to our shores, and they will come sooner than we think. Perhaps our sons and daughters—or even we—may be counted among the martyrs of the 21st century.

We cannot sit and wait in fear, however. We must go to the strongholds of the enemy and engage evil in the power of the Holy Spirit. Hopeless captives must be freed, those who are cast down must be lifted up, the hungry must be fed, those in prison must be visited, and those who are weak and sick unto death must be strengthened.

In the power of the Holy Spirit we can lift them up and empower them so that they will know they are not the victims of history but are actors in a great drama. The story by which we live is the story by which we will die. This is the judgment of God that proves His justice.

Jesus' whole life was a revelation of His pouring out of Himself on behalf of others. Therefore, Calvary was the logical end of his life. He had come to give His life for the sins of the world. He had come to seek and to save the lost. And that is how He lived His life.

If we live a life of avoidance, selfishness and cultural accommodation, we will die that way. Our death will not be a self-offering to God, a final act of worship; rather, it will come as another frustrating interruption, a surprising intrusion into a life that we think is otherwise controlled.

Jesus tells us that if we would find our life we must lose it (Matthew 16:25). We must commit our lives daily into the hands of the Father, trusting that by the Spirit we too can make an offering of ourselves that will glorify God (see Hebrews 9:14).

Our lives tell our testimony—our story—loudly and unmistakably. In a world of competing stories we must tell ours in the context of the story of Jesus Christ, the center of human history and the center of our lives.

Every day we are writing our last will and testament, and bequeathing it to someone. We must bequeath the riches of grace, love, strength and wisdom God has given into our hearts.

Will we allow the evil world and its busyness to "shut down" our story? Will we continue to promote church programs that, unfortunately, leave no time for deep, meaningful Christian fellowship and instead, leave people feeling alienated from each other?

Will we squander our riches, then leave the remains to unappreciative, spoiled relatives who will squander it frivolously? Or will we pass them on to the grateful and faithful ones who have walked and shared our stories?

We must first reclaim our own testimony. We must tell the holy stories of God's way with us to those about us. We must reclaim our local churches as places of personal fellowship. Each local church has a story, a history, a place in God's mission.

Each of us has a story to bring to that mission. Our purposes in stories should be fitted into the purpose and story of that local congregation. Every local congregation should become a place where those who have no family can come into the family of God and interpret their daily lives in the light of God's light.

We must also reclaim our families. Each family must claim a family heritage of grace and goodness. If you do not have a Christian family, then you must find a Christian family in and among the people of God. We need spiritual fathers and mothers, sisters and brothers and children. All of these are in the body of Christ.

The church as a family, and each family within the church, must find ways to honor a holy calling and the gracious gifting of God in each other's lives. We do this through the everyday, ordinary events of laughing and loving and weeping and serving and growing together in the grace of God.

We have a story to tell that is the greatest story ever told. And it is true. The story is under greater attack than ever before, but it is spreading faster than ever before! It is about you and me and everyone else. At the center of it all is God himself, the author and finisher of our faith.

The last chapters of the story are being written now.

Reclaim your testimony.

Become a grateful, holy, powerful actor in this great drama of redemption!

Endnotes

[1] Philip D. Kenneson & James L. Street, _Selling Out the Church: The Dangers of Church Marketing_ (Nashville: Abington Press, 1997) 127, 128.

[2] Stephen L. Carter, _The Culture of Disbelief : How American Law and Politics Trivialize Religious Devotion_ (New York: Harper Collins, 1993) 23, 24.

[3] Edith Schaeffer, _Affliction_ (Grand Rapids, MI: Baker, 1993) 63.

[4] Cited by A. J. Conyers in _Eclipse of Heaven: The Loss of Transcendence and Its Effect on Modern Life_ (South Bend, IN: St. Augustine's Press, 1992) 121.

[5] Kenneson and Street, 71.

[6] Harry Blamires, _Secularist Heresy: The erosion of the Gospel in the Twentieth Century_ (Ann Arbor, MI: Servant Books, 1980) 41.

[7] Neil Howe and William Strauss, _Millenials Rising: The Next Great Generation_ (New York, Vintage Books, 2000) 7.

[8] Edwin H. Young, _Purpose of Suffering: Knowing the God Who Comforts_ (Eugene, OR: Harvest House, 1985) 133.

[9] Harold S. Kushner, _When Bad Things Happen to Good People_ (New York: Avon Books, 1981) 67.

[10] Brennan Manning, _Ruthless Trust: The Ragamuffin's Path to God_ (San Francisco: Harper, 2000) 34.